# THE
# MINISTER'S HELPER
# MANUAL

## PASTOR MICHAEL C. CHAMPION, SR.

**author**HOUSE®

AuthorHouse™
1663 Liberty Drive
Bloomington, IN 47403
www.authorhouse.com
Phone: 833-262-8899

Published by AuthorHouse  08/19/2020

ISBN: 978-1-7283-7061-3 (sc)
ISBN: 978-1-7283-7108-5 (e)

Library of Congress Control Number: 2020916228

*I dedicate this book to my Mom - Mrs. Grace Bennett - A true woman of God. Momma, now as a man I understand the enemy cannot touch you. Eighty-two years of anointing.*

*To my lovely wife Carla: You are the single human guiding force that makes me want to be all I can be in Christ. A true Champion.*

*To my mentor who is deceased - Malik - Thanks for the faith in me and I remember your words.*

*Anything you survive in life, the lesson learned is the blessing earned.*

*To my children: You are the best ever.*

*Thanks Charlie for all the good conversations.*

*Also a very special thanks to my church family.*

*Pastor Michael Champion*
*aka Champ*

# FOREWORD

What you are holding in your hand represents the commitment of a person deeply concerned with the serving actions of every Christian in ministry and helping them finding their best and highest functioning level. Pastor Michael C. Champion has immersed himself into the perils of urban ministry for over 35 years and possesses rich insights into the benefits practical wisdom, humility and proper decorum offers every believer in ministry. This compact book of helps is a "helper manual" offering practical guidance by the voice of one which aims to help aid and give prudence. As iron-sharpens-iron let the advice offered in this manual become your sidekick, your deputy, adjunct and helper.

Consider what God has ordered and/or is, ordering for your future? Reading Mark's gospel introduces us to the Old Testament's foretelling of, an unknown emerging "voice of one ... " (Mk 1.3) John the Baptist. The voice of the Baptist becomes the primary agent in the preparation of the way for the Son of God. As the preparer of the way, his is a voice and agent helping, another in ministry. In doing so, John the Baptist passes his torch (ministry) of victory to Jesus to help realize what the Father has ordained for His Son. I say torch of victory, despite his troubles, tribulations, trials, temptations, test and times. John the Baptist did declare his own help (efforts) in the role God had assigned for him saying," ... I indeed have baptized you with water ... " but he speaks this about himself, only in contrast to the greater help (the Son of God) Jesus has promised to administer each of us for our own triumphal victory, by the Holy Ghost.

Like John the Baptist, the voice of Michael C. Champion can be clearly heard in this manual crying out to those of us in minis try to accept his experiences, his torch of victory, his trials, tribulations and tests by way of his voice piercing through this manual helping each of us. Use this book to advise you in your everyday affairs in ministry. Let its voice be a guiding voice and its torch become a familiar torch you utilize to ensure you ultimately triumph along life's journey in ministry God has ordered for you.

David W. Stokes,
Senior Pastor, Temple of Judah
Church of God in Christ

# CONTENTS

# CHAPTER 1

# CONVERSION

Every person who utters 'I am saved', or 'God has called me' must have a genuine conversion or changed life. There is a word associated with conversions called spurious. The word spurious means not being what it purports to be; false or fake; apparent but not actually valid.

Two scriptures support this: *St. Luke 6:43-44* (For a good tree does not bear fruit. For every tree is known by his own fruit.) And *St. Mark chapter 4. Versed 3-7* (spurious fruit) and/or *verse 8* (spurious fruit vs. good fruit).

A) Your conversion should have a history: date, witnesses and testimony from others.

B) If conversion is recent, once must wait on ministry.
   *1 Timothy 3:6, 1 Peter 5:5-6, Romans 12:7*

C) Conversion is a sign of a changed heart and mind and behavior.
   *2 Corinthians 5:17, 1 Peter 4:7-11*

When one is converted, a change takes place on the inside, *(2 Corinthians 5-17)* and shows up on the outside.

A person who has truly been converted begins to seek God or learn about Christ and the Holy Spirit. *1 Peter 2:1-3,* and hungers for a deep relationship with his creator; something they didn't have before conversion. *1 Corinthians 2:13-14*

Once a person has been converted, a spiritual awakening takes place, and baptism is a necessity. *Acts 8:26-39* Since conversion is the entrance to the kingdom of God, the converted person's spiritual life takes on a whole new meaning; the mind changes. Jesus, upon talking to Nicodemus in

*John, chapter 3*, told him that conversion was necessary to experience God's power. You may remember the outcry in Acts 2 from the populace: "What must we do to be saved ?" The reply from Peter was 'Believe on the Lord Jesus Christ and you will be saved.'

In our current world today many people are not converted. Astoundingly, even people in our churches are masquerading as if they have been converted, but they have not. It is our job as ambassadors for Christ to echo was is said in *Isaiah 58:1*. Tell the unconverted; let them know there is a remedy for sin – His name is Jesus. His request is repent, with the results of peace, joy and eternal life.

When a person comes to Christ and accepts Him as Lord and Savior a conversion process must take place. St. Luke 22:31 shows Peter's conversion experience. St. John 3 tells us Jesus shared a born-again conversion experience with a curious Nicodemus. Conversion equals changed mind, lifestyle and religious belief.

When a minister preaches the word of God it is with the purpose that it will reach the lost souls that have not yet been converted, and convert them.

*(Psalms 51:13) (Matthew 18:3)*

In the process of converting to Christianity, one goes from being a sinner to a saint, unsaved to saved. If a person is to be a part of the kingdom of heaven, conversion is necessary.

# CHAPTER 2

# SERVING IN MINISTRY IS A MUST

What does it mean to serve?

Serving God is serving His creation thus glorifying God the father. Serving God is really the essence of worshipping Him. Submission in all ways. [O.T.] *Genesis 27:29, Exodus 3:12* [N.T.] *Matthew 4:10-11, Mark 1:13, Mark 10:45, 1 Corinthians 12:5, Philippians 2:17.*

> A) Many Ministers, especially younger, untrained ministers don't understand 'hands-on-ministry'. Meaningful work [O.T.] Ezra 4:24, 5:8, 6:7 [N.T.] Luke 22:7-13, John 13:13-17 (prime example)
>
> B) Serving involves denial of self and humility. When one serves, one is not always doing what one wants to do but what is needed. St. Luke 5:4-8

Serving is not to be performed with a heart of thanksgiving and gratitude, remembering that the Lord Jesus Christ often divested himself to serve mankind. St. Luke 22:27

It is also great honor to serve. Serving involves a willing heart and mind and a love for service to God the Father's creation. Even God himself to serve mankind. St. Luke 22:27

It is also a great honor to serve. Serving involves a willing heart and mind and a love for service to God the Father's creation. Even God himself serves us. St. John 12:26 – Serving is a high honor in the spiritual realm.

To serve is true worship of God the Father. It demonstrates submission, willing ness and a sign of obedience on both parts – the place of the servant and also those being served. Ephesians 6:5-9

David realized the honor pf serving. Psalms 84:10

Serving also requires a particular thought process. Psalms 100:2 Remember it is a great honor and privilege, and a future reward to one of the Living God's servants.

# CHAPTER 3

# ACCOUNTABILITY

What is Accountability?

Accountability is another requirement in ministry. It means giving permissible access to ones actions or decisions; such as parents are held responsible for children's actions. When anyone allows him or herself to be accountable to a person or an organization, it show honesty, integrity, and humility, not pride.

When one is accountable, one accepts responsibility for their actions, behavior, "The 3 C's" – Character, Conduct, and Conversation. Biblically, God always has an order and His order reflects accountability. The Disciples were accountable to Jesus. (Read St. Luke chapter 10:1-2,17-20)

When one is accountable one is willing to allow others to review their actions – "The 3 C's" - Character, Conduct, and Conversation.

Character is important because it puts the individual on display for all to observe. The attributes of character are the mental and moral dualities of an individual. It shows strength, weakness, personality and reputation. Job 1:8, 1 Corinthians 15:33.

Promotion comes with accountability. In the book of Job chapter 1, verse 8, God speaks of 5 great things regarding Job's Conduct, Character and Conversation. But chapter 2 verse 3, God honor his constant stance of holiness and adds the word integrity. In other words, Job was working with a lot of good, godly attributes.

Accountability shows a willingness to be checked or cross-examined to find out about ones actions, (Psalms 139:23-24), and puts a person in a position for evaluation for promotion, discipline, or reproof. The Bible states in 2nd Chronicles 16:9 that God is searching for individuals who have excellent accountability, to reward them for the position.

It pays to be accountable. It helps to keep us from making bad mistakes or doing harmful things, because we have opened ourselves up for reproof. Accountability is just as good as having a bank account with money. The book of Romans 4:13-23 tells us that Abraham's faith in God gave him faith account. Read the passages for the full benefits of accountability.

# CHAPTER 4

# CREDENTIALS MUST BE GENUINE

Many people in ministry – the secular world – have credentials that are fake, unsubstantial and/or counterfeit.

Credentials are a privilege and honor to possess. There are many kinds of credentials – licenses, degrees, diplomas, doctorates – but many of these credentials have not been earned. They have been stolen, faked, bought. These are simply pieces of paper with ink on them-not worth the paper they're printed on. How can one openly display, use or show a fraudulent document with honest pride?

Jesus authenticated His Disciples with training and sent out to preach and perform miracles. When a document is authentic, it can be validated. It proves or shows the earnest, honest efforts of the responsible holder. The Bible shows us people who used counterfeit credentials and were unsuccessful. –Acts 19:11-19. This clearly shows that fake authority profits nothing. Verse 17 tells how the seven sons of Sceva were totally defeated and exposed for their counterfeit documents.

Genuine Credentials Get genuine Results

Credentials are necessary in today's world with so much corruption, fraud and hedonism; pleasure-seeking people will use any means necessary to exploit other people for their own gain.

Here's a quick metaphor: If you were seriously ill and you heard about a local surgeon whose record with surgery was 100%, and his claim to fame was experimenting on small animals and creatures with a 100% success rate. But at the same time you were referred to a physician who graduated from medical college at the top of his class (Summa Cum Laude) and was a resident at John Hopkins Hospital, which would you choose to operate you? That should be a no-brainer. The second doctor who was a resident at John Hopkins because he has been genuinely accredited. Credentials also show a willingness to not only learn but be taught; a humility of sorts.

Do not seek out fake credentials (from the internet, certain print shops or any illegible way, order-on-line without-necessary-schooling, etc.) One must give him or herself to a legitimate corporation or organization, or accredited organization if possible. Then one can earn an 'educational status'. These credentials that benefit both parties, do not precede the call in ministry. One must have a calling from the most high God and then he or she can seek the necessary credentials to further their ministry.

Personally, I am always a little suspicious of people who too quickly want to enter the ministry and say that God has called them. Whom God calls He qualifies. Amen. So it is a great achievement to gain legitimate credentials, and once you have them the sky is the limit, because you have labored for the necessary qualifications to extrapolate, or pontificate, or expound the Word of the Living God. Seek to be all you can be.

My motto is: In Christ one can dare to be great.

# CHAPTER 5

# EVANGELISM IS A MUST

Matthew 28:19

I am appalled at how many so-called preachers, evanIgelists, apostles, bishops, and missionaries who don "t think its necessary to witness to lost or hurting people. IChrist himself commanded His disciples to go into all the world and make disciples (learners and doers of God's logos or written word.)

Evangelism is the tool to help un aved, hell-bound sinners come to Christ. A person does not know they need to be saved unless they know they are lo t. When it comes to witnessing or evangelizing a person does not have to have a doctorate, degree or even a title.

All he or she has to have is a born-again personal ex perience with Christ, an unction of the Holy Spirit and Ia burden for lost souls. And so having said, where are all of the foot soldiers? Interestingly enough the Jehovah witnesses, the Nation of Islam and the Monnon Church seem to be putting us to shame when it come to evangelizing the world up close and personal. You. me or someone else needs to be about our Father's business and go and proclaim the Good New to a dying hell-bound lost world. Will you go? It is necessary for kingdom advancement.

# CHAPTER 6.

# WHAT TO DO IN THE PULPIT OR HOW DO I ACT IN THE PULPIT

Pulpit. The English word (KJV Nehemiah 8:4) is equivalent to the Hebrew Migdal; a common word for tower. Mo t commonly a raised wooden platform. In the passage of Nehemiah he was delivering the word of God to God 's people. The scene was a raised platform with a wooden podium or pulpit.

In essence, the pulpit as we know it is a place where men and women of God proclaim God's word.

The pulpit is a symbol of power; it displays authority, holiness and sanctity.

When a minister enters a pulpit, they should be designated to do so by responsible Godly officials. When a minister enters a sanctuary we should not always look for pulpit access. I have been a minister for 35 years and have noticed a real lack of reverence for that sacred place knows as the pulpit area.

Upon enteri ng any Holy place one should think about Moses at the burning bush *(Exodus 3:1-5)* or Aaron's on *(Leviticus 10:1-3)*, or even Eli 's sons *(1st Samuel 2:12 & 22)*. The office of a minister has Holy obligations and God requires holiness from all who enter the position. So when any minister has the opportunity to enter a pulpit they should consider it because of what it represents. It is more than a wooden or plastic or metal lectern, it is God's office for delivering His Holy word.

When you come upon a pulpit, look at it as an encounter with God and His Holy people. When Nehemiah stood at the pulpit he had several assistants near him. *(Nehemiah 8:4-5)*. Notice he knew them all by name.

The pulpit is a place of prominence; it is a place where holy men and holy activities occur. When one has access to the pulpit he or she should be mindful of it awesomeness. Upon being a participant in this place be mindful of the reason you are there. A minister's behavior in the pulpit should still be one of servitude. It is not a place for entertainment, self-grandstanding, foolishness or unruly behavior. It is a place of reverence.

Be mindful of the program that is already in place. Make yourself available for service just by your presence and not asking to do anything unless asked by those responsible for pulpit activities

When sitting—Men—please-good posture and alertness to what's going on is necessary. Women should be appropriately dressed, not provocatively or alluring but modestly. *(1ˢᵗ Peter 3:3-4)* Men are not to have roving eyes and lustful looks at females. Men who show these types of behavior are displaying the behavior of false prophets *(Jude 16-19, 2ⁿᵈ Peter 2:12-17)*.

The pulpit is a place of service. Always perform only what is asked of you. If you are asked to pray, just pray, don't pray and then testify. If they ask you to read a scripture, don't read a scripture and pray too. If asked to make remarks, 3 to 5 minutes is very appropriate. Remember if your behavior is correct you will be asked to come back. If not you might just have blown a golden Godly opportunity for ministry.

When you ascend the platform be cordial to all other guests. Please do not draw unnecessary attention to yourself. Don't clown around or make a scene if asked to make remarks after the keynote speaker—do only that; make a few short, respectful remarks. Do try to get up and preach behind him. Believe me, everyone will take notice and it will make you look very uncouth or bad. Don't request special seating unless you are handicapped or seriously ill. No slapping 5's or turning flips—No Foolishness! Always honor the pastor and his wife. Acknowledge speakers and other ministers. When it comes to offering, give the best you can at all times. Be thankful and grateful that God has chosen you to represent Him and be counted as one among the saints. Never sleep in the pulpit (you shouldn't sleep in church anyway) and never enter medicated.

Never enter a church or place of worship expecting to sit in a pulpit. The pulpit doesn't make a minister. Be considerate and be willing to step aside if asked when another person is invited up. Better to step down than be put down. *(James 2:1-4)* The pulpit is a place of honor and privilege for holy men and women of God.

Now that I have been born again and entered the Kingdom, and God through Christ has specifically chosen me, I am moving into the position of a herald, or a voice crying in the wilderness of this sinful world. How do I approach such a pure, powerful, sanctified station? Easy. Put yourself in Brother Moses' shoes when approaching that holy standing place. He first listened to God's instruction, *Exodus 3:5.* Moses had to prepare to approach that sacred place with preparation, or God's instruction: Remove any hindrance to keep me from having intimate contact with your whole being. Shoes off, so can touch you the way I made you. I want you to reverence the place you are about to stand and I need your person. Nothing you picked up along the way: shoes, shirt, covering,—nothing. I want to empower you, not anything you have. I want to touch you one on one. So when you stand in the holy place to deliver, you will have been touched by my person and will be able to speak what I say—do what I do—and represent the true God of Israel. Because naked you came into the world-no extras-and I need you fully, wholly, just you. It will be you l use. The stick l gave you is just a prop, the brother I gave you just a helper. When you stand in the holy place, you will deliver the Dunamis and Exousia word because you will have stood on holy ground, and what comes from you will be the holiness you stood on, the holiness that you will deliver. So when you stand in God's pulpit, be sure your walk equals your talk, your words are His words, your faith His faith, and don't worry about what to say. Remember He made the tongue, and even though you may be 'degreed up', I 'preach-gifted up', or 'anointed up', God himself will give you what to say in that very moment, that very hour. But remember, **it's not what you do in the pulpit. It's what God does through you in the pulpit.**

# CHAPTER 7

# YOUR WORD, GIFT AND ANOINTING MUST BE FROM GOD

When you as a minister have an opportunity to proclaim The Word, the # 1 rule is: Make sure it is strictly from the Bible—Genesis through Revelations. Be prepared—always pray before speaking; the word you speak must be spirit-anointed. Anybody can talk, lecture or converse, but preaching is a God-given gift. If a person has truly been called by God to extrapolate His word evidence will be proved by the fruit of his lips.

Preaching God's word is the greatest thing any man, woman, boy or girl could ever do. *Jeremiah 23:29* God likens His word as fire (a purifier) or a hammer (an instrument of power). So, handling the word of God must be done in God's power.

The word of God is the greatest force in the universe. All words secular and social have the ability to motivate, change, educate people, but God's word supersedes all. This is because His word gives life to anyone who hears it. His word is also a seed; so all preachers are like Johnny-Apple-Seed planters. Plant the seed of God's word and it will surely grow.

Not only should a preacher speak the word of God but they should live it. *James 1:22-25* tells us to put some action to our talking: if your walk doesn't equal your talk, then you should be silent until God quickens, then speak and act on His word.

All men have gifts but we are talking about spiritual gifts. Some men and women in the world can sing, I some dance, some write, act, cook, sew-but these are natural gifts or talents. A gift is a natural and God given ability to perform something meaningful or useful. Ln God's kingdom our gifts are to be used and shown to people. **These gifts are God-given and should be used to His glory.**

Gifts also compliment each other. A preacher can be inspired by a good soloist. A Sunday school teacher I can motivate children to excel in personal life and social life. The Bible also says ones giftedness can make I room for the gifted one. *Proverbs 18:16*

How do I know if I am gifted?

I think when a person has a spiritual gift God allows people to encourage the gifted one to exercise or use the particular gift they have been endowed with. The beauty of a gift is it is from God Almighty.

Moses had the gift of leading. Abraham had the gift of faith. Barnabas had the gift of consolation. Paul had the gift of determination; he was a great finisher.

Giftedness can provoke jealousy and envy. It is a special person who realizes that even though they may be gifted, it is from God. *James 1:17 1st Timothy 4:14*

**Gifts are to be used to glorify God help people and show God as the creator.** All of us have different gifts. *Romans 12:6* A person can also perfect their gift; the more a person exercises it, the greater if impact will be.

Anointing fall on me— Anointing fall on me - is a song that has been echoed for years.

What is Anointing? How does one get Anointed?

Anointing is a very loosely used term in today's ecclesiastical circles. The original use of the word anointing pointed to three classes of people: Prophets, Priests and Kings. The word Mashalt (Strong's Concordance #4886), in the Old Testament Elisha was commissioned and anointed in 1st *Kings 19:16*. David was anointed.

What is mostly referred to, or associated with an anointing is the act of the operation of the Spirit of God or Holy Spirit; in the (N.T.) a Greek word (Chrio) [Strong's #5548].

Christ was described as having this anointing with the Spirit of God for His ministry and in the Old Testament. *Isaiah 6 1:1.* Christ was equipped with the supernatural ability to perform miracles; break strongholds, cast out demons, control nature, etc.

A person 's anointing is like a perfume fragrance. A fragrance is a smell that attracts people to a certain individual. In the Bible perfume represents either seduction or influence. Like a good perfume, anointed people attract others because they are attractive in more way than one. Just a few attributes of an anointed person help to handle the word of God powerfully, and effectively. Use any gift you may have—(when ministering, healing or casting out demons)—singing, playing an instrument, evangelizing, praying—these a just a few way to help the anointed person stand out from those that are not, but in need of the anointed one.

You can be an anointed influencer, introducing people to God and His kingdom. When one is truly anointed you must be "dead" to all your selfish needs; ambitions, popularity, pleasure-seeking, filthy lucre, greed, unrighteous gains, etc.

Remember this Golden Nugget:

The validation of your calling is not the applause of people, not ministry results, not education or the pleasing of men. The true anointing is God's approval and validation of you. In other words, God's presence being with you and in you and using you is the focus and ammunition of the anointing.

Another aspect of the anointing is it can be transferrable. Read *2ⁿᵈ Kings chapter 2* to get a clear understanding.

The anointing of God comes at a great price: death to self, trials, difficulties, and perseverance. If you want to be anointed stay close to Christ; stay in your word, stay in constant prayer and your anointing will be effective and recognized.

# CHAPTER 8.

# STYLES OF PREACHING

The word 'Preach' is a simple but powerful word in Christianity. A preacher should always have a message from God.

God reveals Himself generally through His word and He uses holy men, women, boys and girls to deliver it.

The Bible talks a lot about preaching & teaching. Your message as a man or woman of God should be to preach sacred doctrine. *2nd Timothy 1:13, Titus 2:*

All preachers are different. Some examples are:

Extroverted vs. Meek
(John the Baptist) (Moses)

Serious Prophet vs. Son of Consolation
(E::.ekie/) (Barnabas)

Fiery vs. Love Talk
(Peter) (St. John)

All of these men had their own style at delivering God's word. But they had one thing in common other than Jesus and the Holy Spirit—They Got The Job Done—They were effective.

Many people wonder what they should preach. **Preach the Word.** *2nd Timothy 4:2*. Preach against sin. Why? Because God hates sin and anything God hates, you as a man or woman of God should preach against it too.

Another style of preaching is Evangelical—preach to save souls.

Pastoral preaching—preach to keep the kingdom principles together. There is nothing wrong with a preacher speaking softly, loudly, charismatic or whooping. Many people of the 21st century have a problem with whooping. I don't have a problem with it—never did—because I realize that this is a unique style that mostly black preachers have developed over the years. 'Whooping' is like putting gravy over chicken and rice or gravy over steak and potatoes: it tastes better-it goes over better. I'm not talking about the preacher who reads 3 scriptures and then whoops and howls for 30 minutes. That's not preaching—that's just plain looney-toons preaching. I've found out as a black African-American preacher/teacher/pastor, that many people have a problem with something because they don't understand it. The solution to that is to get an understanding as to why the preacher is doing what he or she is doing. I've also found that young people especially what to change things, or re-invent the wheel. I remember when a good sized wheel was 13" or maybe 15" or 16", but they've taken wheels to another level—(22-26-dubs), they don't realize it is still just a wheel.

People want real talk, though I've found out that many enjoy a good 'whoop' out of a preacher—it stirs up the emotions; makes a person feel like talking back to the speaker, makes them want to shout. But just like any thing else there are some who hate 'whooping'. These I are the people who just want to go to church and not feel anything. They don't want anything from God, just to be a spectator. But I have learned that when a preacher says he/she really hates whooping, its because they can't or don't know how to 'whoop'. If you can't whoop and want to whoop, ask God. *1st John 3:22. St. John 14:13-14.* I've personally had a disagreement with a young I preacher about 'whooping', because he said it's not necessary. I told him I would give him a $100 bill if he I could whoop-just start whooping right here right now. He kept saying he could, but I left with my $1 00 bill.

*"I say Yessss—he will-will-will-will make a way! Can I get a w·itness—ah ya-ya-ya-ya-ya . . ."* You get the rest. Don't knock it till you try it. People

can be saved whether you whoop or not. Just preach it. A preacher doesn't have to whoop if he doesn't want to or can't, but if he says he's representing God, he'd better PREACH.

Another style of preaching is educational systematic preaching. I personally like this style because so much can be communicated. But a person has to have a mind to hear what the spirit is saying to the church, and good ears also when this type of preacher is preaching because he is saying something, many things, but you must be "hungry"-ready to receive.

Last but not least is the charismatic guru who can talk dollars out of your pockets. Beware—this preacher's tongue is so smooth he can make a snake bite itself! These preachers always have a "key word" or phrase— for example there may be 150 people in a room and he'll say, "Somebody in this room needs a job" and 15 people scream 'Yes'! Well of course he can say that with the unemployment rate so high. They ha e prayer lines, but their lines have price tags—$50 line, $100 line, $500 line—but I don't hear no faith line.

The bottom line is—watch out.

# CHAPTER 9

# SERVICES

(BAPTISM. REVIVALS, ORDINATIONS, WEDDINGS, ETC.)

A Minister is strictly a servant for God Almighty. In ministry or the ecclesiastical field, we are Clergy. It is our job to perform many tasks for the general populace or church body. For services such as baptism, wedding, ordinations, the person officiating the ceremony should be licensed, ordained and in good standing with his or her church, especially the Body of Christ.

Baptism is a holy rite, weddings are a sacred service, and ordinations of deacons and/or ministers are holy also. A minister should be saved, learned, and account able. *Romans 8:29-30.*

Many services in the body of Christ do not require licensed, ordained or super-educated persons, but these are still very important and needed services, such as Sunday School Teachers, Nurses, Youth Aides, Bible study and prayer meetings leaders, etc. These require saved and sanctified people. In today's era, many people who want to operate in the Body of Christ don't feel or think it is necessary to be trained or groomed to perform many of these duties, but that is not okay.

The service(s) being performed—whatever it is—requires knowledge, experience and humility. Take baptism for example. When someone is baptized I'm sure that they believe that the person administering the ceremony is qualified and righteous in their personal and spiritual life.

Weddings need to be done by a licensed, certified minister. I rarely marry a couple who will not take premarital counseling. Counseling is absolutely necessary because this may be a first-time experience for both, or one of the parties may be divorced; its possible that neither one has a clue of what marriage really is. Therefore a learned and qualified minister should be on deck to help the couple out. When a minister is asked to help out with other service : eulogies, hospital visits, ordination services of deacon or ministers should be done by a person who is already certified.

Serving is one of the most important parts of the Christian Ministry and if a person has the opportunity Ito get schooling or any type of helpful 'grooming', one should jump at the chance. God wants his people to be prepared. *Hosea 4:6* So, just as the motto of the Boy Scouts is 'Be Prepared', a godly man's motto is be prepared also. *2ⁿᵈ Timothy 4:2*

It is a privilege to be able to serve and minister to God's people. People who have been converted and are new to the Body of Christ need to be guided by experienced and trained men & women of God. The

services we perform are for people that are spiritual and have a deeper desire and need to get close to God the Father.

We have been chosen and given this great opportunity I to make disciples. Matthew 28:19. So at every opportunity we must do our best and let the Spirit of The Holy One do the rest. Serving is a prerequisite to going to heaven. *Revelation 14:13.* The service men and women will someday rest and their reward awaits them.

Serve with all of your might. It is an achievement like no other. People will take notice. God will take notice I and heaven stores up your notices.

# CHAPTER 10.

# FELLOWSHIP AND WORSHIP

One of the commands Christ left for u to do mightily was to fellowship. *St. John 13:35*

True fellowship has the essence and flavor of love. Fellowship is needed in the Body of Christ because we are one body.

The word fellowship means to have friendly association with other people. Many people shy away from fellowship. I wish I could give you all of the reason they do, but the truth is I just don't have all of the answers. But here are a few: some are just anti—social, others are ashamed of their appearance/have low selfesteem, or others just plain don't know how. But if one is to be a part of the church body they need to learn the art of fellowship.

Fellowship has lots of benefits, such as: friendship, help when needed, and support—especially after a tragedy such as loss of a loved one, being diagnosed with a terminal illness, divorce, fire, flood,—all of these involve fellowship.

The word 'fellowship' comes from Greek and the meaning of the word is actually about a boat or 'ship' with lots of 'fellows' rowing and turning the ship. All of them in the same boat (some happy, some sad), but all together "fellow-shjpping".

Fellowship is not as easy for everyone as it is for some, but it is a must in the church family. A picnic has fellowship, a church anniversary, fundraiser, even regular church worship involves fellowship.

Worship is different from fellowship because it demands the awesomeness of God—the commitment of all people who desire to pay homage. Psalm 100:1-2 says make a joyful noise unto the Lord, all ye people, I which implies more than just one person. Worship can be done anywhere it has a point of contact; where all are in close proximity giving God his glory.

Worship is an experience like no other. When we I come to worship service, no matter what position you're in or not in, feeling good or not so good, sleepy or lazy, worship should be given to God. Worship is a personal expressive experience done by an individual or group of individuals. Worship is a human response to the perceived presence of The Divine. This presence is above normal human activity and this presence is absolutely holy.

How does one worship?

It involves some religious activity such as praying, singing, preaching, fasting, giving thanks, teaching, dancing. Corporate worship is found in many place in scripture such as (O.T.) *Exodus 5:1, 1 Kings 8:54-66,* (N.T.) *Hebrews 10:25, Revelation 11:16.*

Worship is the highest adoration any person can be involved in when it comes to showing God full reverence. Anyone should be able to worship God anytime, anyplace.

# CHAPTER 11

# PERSONAL, SPIRITUAL DEVELOPMENT OF ONE'S SELF

When it come to a person being fit for the kingdom, one must do self-inventory of every area of his or her life. *1 Timothy 4:8* echoes these words: bodily exercise profits little but godliness is profitable to us all. Here is an introspective look into how fit you are as a servant/soldier. In St. *Luke 9:62*, Jesus speaks to the man who would be a follower, but instead wants to stay and bury his father. Jesus shared some mighty stern words: Any one, having put their hand to the plow, and looking back, is NOT FIT for the kingdom of God. It require serious commitment.

One can be fit with a sure calling that him or her studies feverishly. Find a mentor or mentors who are experienced in the Word Of God and ministry so one can glean and sharpen themselves for ministry. One can develop a serious prayer life. *St. Luke 18:1*

Time is also an important factor. Time of word preparation. Joshua was told in chapter one to meditate day and night, to observe and walk it out. Personal preparation involves denying of ones self. One can be given to fasting. Fasting is an excellent and powerful tool in the spiritual realm. But one must take the risk to gain the benefit. I started out right away after my new birth and baptism experience, and was joined by a brother who was a new convert and we immediately began to fast. We were literally taking God at His word to see some results. And results we got. At that point in time, my life was brazen faith. We started out with 3—day fasts-nothing but liquids. This went on for about a month once a week. Our countenance lightened—we were more deserving. One of our friends who had smoked cigarettes since he was 9 years old joined in on one of the fasts and hasn't smoked another cigarette in 34 years. Praise a Holy God!

We next moved to 7 day fasts with just liquid, and man, what a new dimension. We would go out witnessing and praying, and ran into all sorts of people (hurt, unsaved, bound), and the Lord allowed us to be very effective. Last but not least, we ventured 14 days. This was the 'Master Blaster'—the ascent of Horeb. We were attempting 14 days with just water, doing basic spiritual principles—praying, witnessing, casting out devils (really!). But around the 11th or 12th day, we called each other on the phone at about the same time confessing we both had just broke the fast minutes apart. But it was a spiritual joy and high I'll never forget as long as I live.

More personal development is to get involved in hands-on-ministry; not always preaching. Volunteering I opens many doors for willing hearts when a servant of the month high God is willing to serve. Social service agencies are a great place to strengthen a spiritual resume. Food pantries, jails, drug treatment centers, nursing homes and hospitals give all of us a great opportunity to develop our lives spiritually. I suggest you try it whether in school, already in ministry, pastor, Sunday school teacher, or just a busy member. Personal spiritual development does the body good.

# CHAPTER 12

# PUTTING ALL YOU'VE LEARNED TO USE

*I've just finished reading eleven other chapters of spiritual jargon. Now I must ask of myself—How does this apply to me? What can I equate to me? Even if I agree or disagree, I have learned some new information. So how do I put it to use?*

#1 . Make sure you learn it and then use what you need the way you might need it. You may have a different outlook on chapter 3, 7 or 9, but don't disqualify the whole book because of a different viewpoint. Reading a book is sometimes like eating fish. Eat the fish but remember to spit out the bones.

I can put to use what I've learned from this book whenever I encounter those situations. I can use it just like it is—if its 'dead-on-the-money' to me, or I can chop it up, slice and dice it and still get the job done successfully.

I need to be thirsty to find the unsaved, the saved. The Protestant, Jew, Gentile, men, women, boys and girls, to get results and watch the stuff I've learned and my help from God, the Holy Spirit and Jesus, and m y great efforts and watch the results. One plants, one waters, God gives the increase. This book is being released in Spring of 2014. Be a part of the crop. Be a part of the harvesters.

*When you own afield, it's great.*
*When you break up the field it's even greater.*
*When you plant seeds in the field—*
*What you got comin' comes up later,*
*And God makes you abound in all your labor.*

# CHAPTER 13.

# MARRIAGE

The greatest union other than God The Father's union with man, has to be marriage. The word union is the action or fact of joining or being joined. In Genesis it was God The Father who joined Adam and Eve together. Genesis 2:21-22. This is literally the first marriage in the history of mankind.

Marriage is the formalization and sanctification of the union between man and woman; the actual honest way of a man and woman getting together rightfully in God's eyes, or we could say 'The Holy Hookup'. Marriage sets the standard for the future and the life of a healthy family. Marriage started out as a relationship between a man (male) and a woman (female). This is the only marriage God recognizes, and I agree with God totally. (Amen) *Matthew 24:35* God's word never will fail. Marriage is the union that God put in place for procreation of the family.

The 21st Century seems to be straying away from God's law about marriage. But God isn't and neither are law-abiding people and Christian believers.

Jesus let us know in his own words about hi Heavenly Father's intention for marriage in *Mark 10:5-9* and *Matthew 19:4-9*. This is the Biblical principle of marriage. Marriage has many benefits: true love, commitment, sex, children's prosperity and God's blessing. The love in marriage is the act of giving ones self to each other for life. In a song by 'The Artist Formerly Known As Prince', titled The Greatest Love Story Ever Told, Prince quotes a very important line that goes like this: *'Why do you think Adam never left Eve—Why? Because it was love, pure love, eternal love, selfless love, godly love.'* Just listen to the song.

God allowed sex for procreation and expressing ones devotion of love. Adultery is forbidden because of the holy commitment, the vow, the contract of love. Marriage demand faithfulness. True faithfulness will not allow in to disrupt the holy union.

## For the Minister

#1 A minister must walk in love and understanding I with his wife.
*1 Peter 3:7*

#2 The wife is to be submissive to her husband.
*Ephesians 5:22*

#3 If there are children they are to obey their parents.
*Ephesians 6:1-2*

All of these 3 statements if followed make for an excellent family, prosperous life and joy unspeakable.

The husband is the head of the wife. The word 'head' in scripture represents authority-not being abused. Neither man nor woman is superior to the other. Men and women are equal in Christ. It is a holy partnership. Both are from each other and the relationship they have comes from God the Father. When God talks about His order he means Christ-man-woman. When it comes to the man and woman it is about functional order.

The male minister must rule his home. 1 Timothr 3:4-5. This means you are the decision maker. You are the priest, provider and protector. But it must be done in love. Your marriage will survive anything if you carefully follow the mandate in *1 Corinthians chapter 13 verses 4-9*. To the married man and to the married woman—remember, God hates divorce. Malachi 2:1 6

Remember a key to a successful marriage is

***"The family that prays together stays together."***

# CHAPTER 14

# MY VOCATION AS A MINISTER

Being a minister is no easy task. If God has truly called you into the Ministry (male or female), give your call due diligence. Do your God-given duty. You must teach and preach the truth. It is okay to teach and speak from other pro-Christian and some secular books, but remember God's word is the final measuring rule.

My motto is show me a person who <u>can read but will not read is stuck.</u>

Ministering and serving go together. A true minister of the Gospel must have a burden for the lost—people do I not know they need to be saved until they know they are lost. When it comes to saving people, in most case the lost will not seek you, you have to seek them. *St. Luke 15:4*

When a man or woman is called into ministry they must work a soon as possible. Reason being Jesus' I own statement in Matthew 9:37. People need help. God is always at work. When I hear people say they are unemployed, I say 'Have you filled out an application with God? God's want ads are never filled'.

A minister must be willing to Live, preach, eat, and teach the Holy Word of God. David said I am thirsty for thee 0' God. *Psalm 42:1*

When a minister ministers it involves correcting. rebuking and exhorting people. *2 Timothy 3:16*

The minister is to be a holy vessel—always working for his master and the kingdom. Live a holy dedicated life to God. The best sermon is not one that is preached but one that is lived.

God chooses every minister after His own will. He is aware of the life to be lived, the mind to be used, the behavior to be acted upon and the satisfaction of the ministry of the one he has chosen. Any man or woman called by the Holy Father of Jesus to serve in ministry must be humbled, dedicated and grateful.

If you bought this book I am quite sure you know the reason, but don't stop here. There are many battles you must win, many souls you must reach, and man y lives you must touch, so continue your God-ordained Journey.

A war is going on that cannot be seen with the human eye, and God has created warriors that are up for the warfare. You must win, you must allow God to lead and guide you every step of the way and at the end of the journey, you can look back at all of the giants that the Spirit of God in you has slain. Look back-you will see them laying by the side of the road defeated by none other than a willing worker of Christ. I say, *'Onward Christian soldier, march right on to war'. Amen.*

# CHAPTER 15

# FAMILY

In the beginning God had a plan for an earthly family. It was somewhat modeled after His heavenly family. When God created the man and then introduced the woman to the man, family was being introduced to all humanity to come.

Family matters (husband, wife, children) represent *Ecclesiastes 4:9*. When the word of God talk about a two-fold cord, it is because two represent a bond of unity. This shows togetherness.

A minister that represents Almighty God has an awesome responsibility to his own family. This responsibility requires loyalty, dedication, godlines . Another one of the responsibilities is love. This love will show in the disposition and actions of the person that is a part of this awesome unity. Family has responsibility to each other as members of this group. A reverence to God the Father should be displayed in thought, word and deed. God has always promoted family. In any community, family is a representative of the Creator. Jesus on many occasions worked with family matters. *St. John 9*. The man born blind. A mother who has lost her only child. *St. Luke 7:11-18*. The death and resurrection of Lazarus. *St. John 11*.

Family is the joy of humanity. As ministers of the gospel we should promote family and Godliness every time we get the opportunity.

Families are supposed to enjoy the fruits of God's creation. Families should pray together, worship together and enjoy life together.

Satan is anti-family. So we must always put God and the sanctity of the family first. Families are meant to reflect God' oneness. Ministers should model God's unity in the earthly relationship that they have with each and every family member.

A true Godly family should mirror God's togetherness. God the Father, God the Son, God the Holy Spirit.

Even though they each function in different capacities, they are still one.

Family unity is what the world—especially this 21$^{st}$ century generation—needs to see. To see the real value of a family, not just any family, but a family who redeems the benefits of God's graciousness.

Family matters to all, whether God's family or the human family. To witness a Godly family is to witness the great beauty of Family.

# CHAPTER 16

# CHURCH IS NOT A BUILDING

The church is more than just a building, it is an organized group of religious believers. The church is a living organism of a Holy God.

Many people think of the church as a building; someplace to go and see or hear from God. Others look at the church as an *Instagram*—a place to get quick solutions for misery and problems. Some people see the church as unfriendly, hypocritical or a money-grabber. Well, their opinion is their own.

The church is a headquarters of God's mighty power, compassion, and a station where anyone willing to seek out the Living God may find Him. It is not a place of only perfect people seeking perfection from a perfect God. The church is a come-as-you-are, but not stay-as-you-are place.

The church building is a public place and anyone is welcome. Almost all churches welcome you with open arms. The reality of it is it is a place I recommend everyone check out. I mean, give the church a real chance. Many come with skepticism and criticism. But come and see what the word of God really says. The church is the foundation of Christ' message. The bible is the flag we wave for all to see.

Love is to be on display and given out to all who come. *Isaiah chapter 55*. The name doesn't matter, the location doesn't matter, race, creed, color, how big or mall the church is, just give it a chance, and I guarantee you will feel a sense of refreshing and the possibility of a brand new start in your own personal life. Remember God is no respecter of people.

I know the church impacted and made a huge difference in my life and the life of all those who give her a true chance. The church is a matter of the heart and I that' what God does—He looks at the heart.

Go to church. Not only does the church need you, but I you need the church. Come with an open heart, open mind and see what God does. I'll tell you what He does. *Psalm 37:4* He will give you your heart's desire. When you open up your heart to him, He opens up His complete self to you. Don't put it off any longer! The church needs you, wants you, is ready for you.

# CHAPTER 17

# ACQUIRING INFORMATION AND WISDOM

We all desire to be all that we can be at any age in life. We must remember that life is a journey and in order to function and have a purpose in life, we need general guidelines, both secular and spiritual. They say we should grow as we go.

I have had the opportunity to watch a bald eagle fly. There is one thing I've noticed about them. They have a majestic and royal essence about them. They don't just fly—they make preparation to fly. Just as an eagle makes preparation to fly so must we make preparation to be wise and soar to success in life. We must prepare to soar in life, and one of the way we soar is to use the blessings that God has endowed us with. For in stance, the brain. It is located at the top of the body in a head protected by a skull, and with ears to receive information about life. If we seek out books, instructors, mentors and friends, but especially God himself, we will soar in life and become acquainted with wisdom.

In the book of *Proverbs chapter 1 verse 2*, there is divine information. First to know wisdom, and instructions to perceive the words of understanding. Ministers - we especially need to tap into this verse because of the power it reveals. Wisdom is having the know how and skill to deal with the task at hand at any given time.

Ask yourself: Is the task you're about to deal with:

A) A Spiritual matter
B) A matter of worldly challenge
C) Personal challenge

No matter what the task wisdom is needed to deal with it.

In order for one to grow one must seek wisdom. A leader cannot teach what he does not know, and he I cannot lead where he does not go.

When I acquire wisdom it is not only for me, it is to be applied to the daily situations of life; to be sponged and communicated to others. Just because I'm smart it doesn't make me wise. Just because I'm prosperous it doesn't make me wise. Wisdom—especially the kind I we need as ministers comes from God. *James 3:13-17*

In the 21st century, the age of challenging changes and thing like B&E (Business & Economics), one has to be wise. Having a faithful ongoing relationship with God is the way to go. I tell all people that God along with education is the sure-fire way to avoid poverty.

Wisdom is the principle thing.

How does one know when they have gotten wise?

They make better choices: they build healthy relationships, they succeed and achieve dreams and goals. Wisdom that comes from God has power with it. Many people in the Bible were wise. *Deuteronomy 34:9*— Nun was wise. *1st Kings 4:29*—Solomon was wise.

Wisdom involves skill, prudence, experience. Wisdom is shown to get desired ends by effective means. Seek wisdom and reap a bountiful reward.

# CHAPTER 18

# PERSONAL GROWTH

Sr. John 15:1-5 talks about connection and the benefits of being rooted in God and Christ, when we accept Christ as our personal Savior and begin to live the life as believers, servants and disciples. We need roots. As every living plant is firmly planted in soil, we as believers need to be planted in the spiritual soil of the Trinity: God the Father, Christ His Son and our Savior, and The Holy Spirit. The importance of being connected like this produces fruit. Fruit in the food world is valuable for nutrition. So we as Christians ought to produce spiritual nutrition to a dying body of people otherwise known as worldly people. We are the light I of the world, we are the salt of the earth, but we are also trees of righteous bearing fruit. *Proverbs 11:30*

Our growth is viable to the prayer Jesus uttered to His disciples in *Matthew 6 verse 11*: Give us this day our daily bread. This bread is the *logo* or The Word of God that we grow by. We are responsible for our own spiritual growth. Many believers are concerned with the spiritual growth of other people. This is not a bad I thing, but it can cause one to de-focus from one's own personal growth and become a fruit inspector of others, when the husband/man/God the Father alone is the source of that. The reason to focus on personal growth not to be a public giant and secluded spiritual midget.

When growing up we used to get our height measured by standing up against the wall, and our parent would mark the growth process. Some grew faster than others, but all grew. The ones that seemed to grow the most were the ones who played sports, exercised, ate very well, and rested well. It showed in their growth process. I believe if we want to measure our spiritual growth, we must use the same practice. Find something that we can measure up against; stretch—practice our spiritual sports of witnessing and evangelizing. These practices will cause us to grow personally by working to do kingdom work and help someone receive the word, the Spirit of God, God's precepts, God's will for their life. Take exercise for example. When a person exercises they must be willing to stretch every muscle and part of the body to get a desired result. Our exercise is a workout. It consists of personal prayer, prayer groups, Bible studies, cell groups. These exercises help deepen our own spiritual bodies and as we seek out partners that want to do these spiritual exercises with us, the results will be seen first to each other. Remember this is personal growth, but it can and should require a partner. Read about the benefits of personal growth in *1ˢᵗ Timothy chapter 4.*

Personal growth in Christ requires discipline, determination, humility and a willingness to be fit for the kingdom of God. This process requires denying oneself, which by the way, is not easy. It can be accomplished with an attitude of gratitude and lots of humility. When reaching this position people will seek you out because you are now able to produce some of the things of the kingdom. Remember this is a personal God thing for you. This is your time to press out anything that will interfere with the growth you need. It will be accomplished through a series of events: I prayer, fasting, fellowship, study, hands-on-ministry. But a great deal of your personal growth will come from introspect and allowing yourself to be crossexamined by other brothers and sisters who are also seeking personal growth in their life with Christ. Also needed are accountability partners who will align themselves with you for the success of personal victory. The personal sacrifices that you value for personal growth will reveal a wealth of personal knowledge and skills that will make you very effective for the journey you're on to build the kingdom.

# CHAPTER 19.

# PRESENTING THE GOSPEL TO MY FAMILY

Many ministers live with the burden of unsaved spouses and children. First remember this is not your fault. The situation just happens to be that way. But there is a solution and you are the vessel to help bring change about. Ministers like to preach sermons but I've learned over the years that the best sermon is one that's lived outright for everyone to see.

I would think that as you read this you remember when you were not saved and someone presented the Gospel of Jesus Christ to you, or God made the opportunity for you to personally receive Christ.

Let's say your spouse is not saved and does not seem to be interested in you or your God. Your question: What do I do? Glad you asked!

#1—Pray without ceasing, fast, anoint the whole house with blessed oil: door knobs, dressers, pillows—and believe God by faith for your spouse's deliverance and salvation. *1 Peter 3:1-2*

Now I know this verse makes specific reference to the wife's transformation of her husband, but a husband and wife are one in the eyes of God when united in marriage, so believe God 's word and if God said it, believe it and that's that.

Please remember to love your unsaved spouse as God loved you when you were in the world without hope and blinded by the enemy. Jesus came to save people I from their sins.

Your wife or husband that is unsaved is counting on you. *1st Corinthians 7:16* reassures us to continue to look to God who is in control of all things. As human beings we are at the beginning looking at the end, but God is at the beginning and the end and He knows the outcome. *Jeremiah 11:29*. So vouch for your spouse with God—the payoff will be well worth it.

Minister also have children. Our responsibility is care, concern, protection and guidance to our young ones, not necessarily in that order. One of my favorite things to see on a warm day is a flock of geese walking across the road with their young hatchlings. They take meticulous watch over their chicks and any approaching predator or danger has to deal with the parents first. Should we be responsible for our children. Moses was adamant about this in *Deut. 4:9-10* and *Deut. 6:6-9*. We must teach our children how to I honor God and obey God. They learn this by keeping the first commandment with a promise. *Deut. 5:16*

We as parents especially ministers, must adhere to *Proverbs 22:6*. We are to instruct our offspring in the fear and admonition of the Holy God. We are to live a life pleasing to God not only to men but before our immediate families every single day. We are to guide, instruct, discipline and love our children. Many of our children have different disposition and behaviors. Well, we are to take it to the Lord in prayer. Pray without ceasing. Love without boundaries. We are to show our spouses and children what love and the ministry is all about. After all, any child of God is responsible for the ministry of reconciliation. Remember your family is your responsibility.

Here are some helpful tips:

A) **Love draws people**. There is an old saying: You can draw more flies with honey than with vinegar, so try love. *Jeremiah 31:3-4*

B) **Be involved in your spouse's and children's lives and activities.** I have seen over and over again when divorce has ravaged a family, men especially desert their children-not all, but many do. Don't let this be the case for you. When a child feel deserted, isolation sets in and children begin to deal with low self-esteem, abandonment, and rejection issues. I know. I have been on both sides of the coin. So stay involved in your children's lives.

C) **Children need both parents to balance out properly.** A woman cannot teach a boy from example to be a man—it is a man's job. A man cannot teach a girl to be a woman by example—it is the mother's job.

D) **Turn knowledge into practice**. Allow your children and spouse to be able to count on you. Beware of broken promises—broken promises can lead to broken dreams.

E) **Listen to your children**. Don't be too busy with your own stuff and trying to make a dollar and close the children out. They need a parent's advice.

Learn how to resolve conflict with your spouse or child. It is said a mind is a terrible thing to waste. Equally a family is a terrible thing to waste also.

# CHAPTER 20

# RELATIONSHIPS

## (MARRIAGE, FAMILY, OR MINISTRY/CHURCH)

Relationship. That intimacy opens up both parties for vulnerability. In order to become a friend, intimate ex changes (stories, secrets) must be revealed, and then you will find out the true value of those who have your best interests at heart, or those who wish you well but all the time hoping you fail. Any type of hurt hurts. Jesus spoke of His departure in *St. John 14*. He detailed it and told His disciples, 'Let not your heart be troubled', knowing the pain of separation from those you love or care about. The "ouch" comes in because of the feeling itself.

When one opens themselves up to another individual it is risky business. One of the details about church hurt or ministry hurt is the lesson is the blessing. Jesus himself knew that one of His disciples would betray Him but he just went on with business as usual because He knew the ouch was coming. I wonder what is more painful; the knowing of the ouch before it comes or the ouch itself when you receive it. Many a person has joined a church fellowship with open arms only to receive a hearty crucifixion before the third day.

This just happens to be the normal way of human existence. People gain knowledge of another brother or sister' marital weakness. The next thing you know they are next in line with an injured spouse or a disgruntled Deacon or Missionary and they are *off to the races* saying 'I'm only human and God will forgive me.' The devil is a lie. This is not what true Christian relationship or friendships should be about.

Many an anoint good, God-fearing pastors have given opportunity to other preachers or ministers, attempting to help them further their ministry by opening up their wallets, homes, pulpits, only later to be betrayed, abused lied to, or the church splits up, all because of the ouch syndrome which must come. We cannot e cape the ouch syndrome because scripture tell us so. *2ⁿᵈ Timothy 2:12*. The ouch syndrome is essential for our spiritual growth.

The scripture says to arm ourselves, that if Christ suffered in the flesh we shall suffer also. *1ˢᵗ Peter 4:1*. When we as believers/ministers are faced with the ouch syndrome we have to remember to look to the hill from whence cometh our help.

Life is a journey. The Bible says there is a time to laugh and a time to cry. When we experience these times, if it is the 'ouch season', just wait for the rain from the laughter season to come back around because it will. *Psalm 30:5* prepares us for the 'ouch season'. Life is a journey and all things work together for God's good in your life. So be encouraged and remember God is in control. He said He will wipe away all tears. So in your 'ouch moment' just remember the joy of the Lord is your strength.

Amen.

# CHAPTER 21

# STUDY (2ND TIMOTHY)

Nobody cares too much for a dummy except ventriloquists. It's only because they get paid for the dummy.

God requires us to learn about Him and we learn many ways but the most important way is through studying His word. Matthew 11:28 tells us about the benefit of study. Study enables the individual to know whatever it is about God's word that he or she will be communicating to others. I know all of the people from Genesis to Revelation who penned or quoted the words in the Bible had to have a history of study—personal, mentor or other sources. They had to study in order to know what they wrote. We study to learn. When we study, we a ministers or lay people set the example for future student or leaders to follow. The Bible tells us in many places about the value of learning or studying God's word. The Bible tells us in *Acts 7:22* that Moses was learned in wisdom and we know that he was reared in the palace of Pharaoh and had access to all I science, history, cultures, and because of this he was exposed to knowledge. Learning is knowledge, knowledge is power.

The scripture introduces us to the curiosity of knowledge in *Genesis 2:9*. Eve was very interested in acquiring knowledge. Eve so much wanted to know that she violated the very command of God to get knowledge.

Ministers and laypersons gain understanding from study and the knowledge they acquire. When a person has put in study time it helps them become familiar with God's person. We are finite beings and we will only be able to handle only so much knowledge. The knowledge we get from study we begin to experience the benefits of what we have learned. Study is a discipline that not everyone has or desires. I believe over a period of time one has to develop an acquired desire to learn. When you begin to learn then you can apply the written scripture to life. Stephen the martyr in chapter 7 of Acts talks a lot about patriarchs and history of the living God and the prophets and prophecy being fulfilled. I love to study the Bible. When you study you need other scholastic tools to help you in your search for knowledge. When a person is a learned person it only helps the student or audience to have more of a trust in what is being said. There are many people who have problems with the world of education. I believe the more a person has learned and knows, the more effective they will be at what he or she does. Jesus was a Jew and He was taught the law and normal life from parents, community and the lawyers of His time. That is why He tells us in *Matthew 11:28* that we should strive to learn. He implores us to take His voice, meaning the task of studying, upon ourselves to learn of the God we serve and it will benefit us immensely. It will not only educate us but we will receive personal peace and relation from the work and desire of study. One can never go wrong when one works on his or her own behalf to be all that he or she can be. Study and excel at all you seek.

# CHAPTER 22

# CORRECTION—INSTRUCTION—DESTRUCTION

We will experience correction and instruction and pray that the only destruction we experience is the destruction of all the negative situations that we experience in life that will attempt to drag us down as ministers, or wipe us out. *Proverbs 1:7* states 'Fools despise wisdom and instruction.' We as ministers read so we can lead. Readers lead—Leaders read. Reading is a must for a true learner. *St Luke 6:40* tells us that the disciple will be just like his teacher if he or she learns that's what disciples do. A part of being instructed sometimes involves correction. When we falter or make mistakes correction is in order. David said in *Psalm119:67-71*—God's correction involved affliction. Affliction is something that causes pain or suffering. The Psalmist says here the pain was beneficial for him. Correction comes in many forms. Sometimes it comes from a parent, a loyal friend, or it can even come from an enemy. People sometimes mistake positive correction for criticism. Criticism is good when it helps you grow as a person. The department stores all have customer service counters. This is the place where sometimes angry, frustrated people bring their complaints—valid or not valid. They can help the organization become a 4-star business just from a little correction or instruction or complaints. Instruction is always to be taken notice of. Take Peter the disciple, when Christ forewarned him of the cock crowing and his ultimate fall. Instruction is to be heeded. The instructor can be a person, an experience or a classroom. People who go to drivers education to learn to drive are taught by driving instructors. People of faith and ministers should quickly learn that the Holy Spirit is an instructor. *St. John 16:13* tells us this.

Norwegian explorer Roald Amundsen was the first I person to discover the magnetic meridian of the North Pole and to discover the South Pole. On one of his trips he took a homing pigeon with him. When he finally reached the top of the world he opened the cage and set the bird free. Imagine the joy of Amundsen's wife back in Norway when she looked up from the doorway of her home and saw the pigeon circling the sky above. No doubt she said 'My husband is still alive'. So it was when Jesus ascended to His Father. He was gone, but what joy when the Holy Spirit entered the room as a dove at Pentecost; the disciples I knew Jesus was alive. That's just what correction and instruction does to a receiver: it is given out like a boomerang but it comes back.

Correction and instruction if received brings many re wards. To refuse brings destruction. *Proverbs 16:18* echoes the sad reward of ignoring both.

Life has its own way of schooling all of us. We began as fledgling infants who grow up in a world of curiosity. We begin to experiment with this and that and soon we learn that we need help if we are to maneuver smoothly throughout life. Help in the form of correction and instruction comes in many ways. Secular school classrooms that teach us scholastically, classrooms where we learn reading, writing, arithmetic. We finish grade school and we experience learning from people—bullies, friends, mentors, parents, and we go to another level-high school, for many-college, and eventually we graduate to adulthood. This is where former instruction and correction really come in to play. Not much 2+2 or ABC's, but real life experiences: jobs, careers, marriages, social activities, addictions, divorce, bills and such. Now is when life's les sons come in handy. A relationship with God is the greatest faction in this area of life, because we have grown to become totally responsible for all of our choices and actions.

I have had many a good instructor and mentor tell me life is what you make it, and I don't think many people truly cash in on the benefits of life. Jesus said in *John 10:10*—'I want you to have an abundant life'. God desires us all to benefit from what He has to offer. I will continue to be a student and learn to apply "Life 101" to all of my endeavors, because life is all so short so make the best of it. Remember, don't self-destruct, but build on a solid foundation. Enjoy life wherever and with whatever you have. Ever heard the quip 'If life hands you lemons, make lemonade'. That is a great statement. Use instruction and correction to gain a more meaningful life. Remember life is what you make it.

# CHAPTER 23

# OUCH

I start this chapter out with scriptures *2nd Corinthians 11:22-28*, *Galatians 2:4* and *St. Luke 22:48*. (Out of Ouch/Echoes of Pain)

These scriptures deal with pain, betrayal and deceit. One of the earliest recollections regarding personal pain is when a child comes forth from a woman's womb and often times upon delivery they were introduced to a slap from a human hand. This my friends, was probably the first sign of ouch but it certainly wouldn't be his or her last.

Pain or hurt as we experience it comes in many ways, but usually we don't expect or see it coming. Especially from someone we cherish or revere highly; albeit in the life of a believer or minister, pain hurt or ouch becomes all too familiar. David made a statement in Psalms 41:9 about a friend who betrayed him. Well, David should know—ask Uriah the Hittite, the loyal friend whom David not only betrayed but murdered.

Yes, all is not fair in love and war.

The thing about friendship and loyalty, whether it be casual, intimate or just general association, it is not a pleasant experience when one is hurt or betrayed.

In our lives we must live with the trust factor. There is I always somebody who we allow ourselves to get too close to, or in on too many of our secrets. When we let someone into the door of our hearts if he or she is not truly our friend, 'ouches' occur. Life as I know it I or understand it now comes with pain and discomfort. When we bring it upon ourselves it really stings.

King David knew the experience first from both ends of the spectrum in *Psalms 41:9*. He mentions a close I friend who fellowshipped intimately with him betrayed him, but the king did the exact same thing to Uriah The Hittite in *2ⁿᵈ Samuel II* . His ouch included murder and adultery. I wonder if he saw it coming; I truly believe in the law of reciprocity. What goes around comes around. What happens when ouches I benefit us, because an ouch can be for our learning. *Psalms 119:67-71* tells about the help of a good ouch. Many times ouches come from relatives, bosses, teammates. These I think hurt the most, because we don't I expect these people to harm us. I now know what an ouch really is. They have purpose and also lots of schooling for us. Band-aids cover physical ouches, and in the life of a minister a spiritual band-aid is the comfort and word of God.

Ouches can be self-inflicted but never totally avoided.

A good ouch is just a part of life. A good ouch can I prevent one from making the same mistakes again.

Jesus Christ hath suffered the biggest ouch of all: Crucifixion. Christ suffered the ouch syndrome by the will of His Father for the greater good of us all. When I you experience an ouch season or moment, try to find out what you're supposed to learn or gain from this unseemly moment. We have all heard the phrase 'No Pain, No Gain'. I guess there is some truth to that. We will all have our moments of ouches, but to God be the glory for our learning.

# CHAPTER 24

# FORGIVENESS

The Bible is the book that expresses the act of forgiveness from a loving, holy, all powerful God to a creation that has fallen away from His original plan. Man, who is God's crown created being, sinned against his maker and was lost, disorganized and out of fellowship with his maker, and God showed up in gracious fashion with total forgiveness. We as ambassadors for Christ must also be agents of forgiveness. All have I sinned and fell short of God's glory.—*Romans 3:23.* Forgiveness is more than just a word it is an act. According to Oxford forgiveness or the act of forgiving is verbal, meaning it is action. It is to let go of an offense.

Question: Can one forgive him or herself?

I personally don't think so. Why? Because the act of 1 forgiveness is performed by another party other than ones self. Forgiveness come into play when an injustice or infraction has occurred, such as 'He didn't have to hurt me like that' or 'Why did they steal from me or us'.

When Adam and Eve disobeyed God in the garden, God could have been merciless and wiped them out of existence. But instead He let go of the offense that was committed against Him and creation and forgave both of them, though both were guilty. He forgave them instantly. He didn't say Let me think about it or Give me a few days, He released them from it immediately. The world we live in today is in need of forgiveness. Why? Because we are so guilty of forsaking God, Jesus Christ's Father. The one who has sustained and provided for us and kept us in order. We have sinned against Him in so many ways. How could we survive without His forgiveness? We sin daily and need a forgiving God. What if God treated us like we treat Him. Could we stand it? No way!

In *Matthew 6:12* the petitioner asks God to forgive them as we forgive others. Notice the forgiveness is requested outside of ones self, not in and of itself. We need forgiveness, and we need to be willing to release others from their faults and offenses no matter what they are, because we reflect God and mirror His image. It is a big deal to be willing to release people from feelings of guilt or sorrow because of an offense committed.

God is always willing to forgive if we just acknowledge our sins. To forgive is to let a person or parties go free, or let the guilty go free, whether guilty or not. It is outside of a person's own power to release a feeling from the offended. Just imagine the thief on the cross at Calvary being forgiven or freed just before crossing over into eternity. God steps in and releases him, sets him free, at peace. Why don't you follow suit and let someone go free. What about that absent father, that abusive mother, that bully brother, racist neighbor, Godless persons. Ask God the Father, 'forgive them for they know not what they do'.

Let the guilty go free in God. He will be the judge, the just judge. But remember He is the forgiver.

# CHAPTER 25

# SACRIFICE

Life is really about sacrifice, such as the animals' blood shed in *Genesis 3:21*. Blood was shed so life could continue. God is the ultimate one when it comes to sacrifice.

Sacrifice involves the bringing of something to a party (person) to express devotion, thanksgiving or the need for forgiveness.

The first mention of humans giving a sacrifice is that of Cain and Able in *Genesis 4*. A sacrifice shows care and concern to a party. When we live our lives, sacrifices must and will be made. Many people have sacrificed their livelihood to raise children to grow up and have a better quality of life; working 2 or 3 jobs to make life a little more comfortable for someone else. I think some of the first sacrifices made are the sacrifices of love to people who are undeserving. By that I mean people who don't value the quality of the existence of life. A sacrificial life is a life that is selfless. I often tell people the scale of beings in life should be measured. God—others—self—seems crazy but that is the way order is balanced. God first committed to His creation and others second. Why? Because God said we should esteem others better than ourselves.

Listen, this doesn't mean we totally neglect our person, but it is God who takes care of us. That is why we echo the phrase 'Give us this day our daily bread'. When we are sustained we can help sustain others. How many people have made sacrifices throughout I history for the good of all mankind, whether Christians or not. Many a heathen have made sacrifices that I made life easier for others. What about plantation owners who lived off the backs and labor of people I forced into hard labor for the unjust benefits of others. Just think about who has made a sacrifice other than

God. I'll bet if you do a serious search you will see a lot of sacrifices have been made for you to get where you are today.

The ultimate sacrifice was the cross at Calvary. God sending His Son in the likeness of sinful flesh to redeem all humanity from the curse. Christ who was a sinless deity volunteered to be a sacrifice for a depraved sinful race of people who really didn't deserve it but was granted it from God. How awesome a feat! It astounds me every time I think about the ultimate sacrifice that was available for me and anyone else who would receive the Son of God.. Sacrifices are a necessary part of life. When was your last sacrifice? Who was it for? For what or whom are you willing to sacrifice? Remember, Jesus paid a debt He did not owe. I owed a debt I could not pay, so He sacrificed and paved the way.

# CHAPTER 26

# LIFE'S LESSON

The school of life has many classrooms. All of us have been students. *John 10:10.* Jesus tells us His desire is for us as believers is to have an abundant life or plentiful life.

Life's lesson began at birth. *Ecclesiastes 3* tells us just a few of the classrooms we must experience. I have learned that as we journey throughout life, when we experience life, all the lessons we learn in the classrooms of life is a blessin'. I mean, in many ways, experience is the best teacher sometimes. Growing up in a dysfunctional family, birth entrance into life can be painful. Classroom #1.

Your environment, your circumstances, can have a great effect on your attitude in life, meaning how far you achieve your goals if you have any. I believe everyone starts out with goals in life. Remember kindergarten – the graham crackers and milk were just a treat for the new journey.

Lessons are automatic if you are alive.

Lesson One: **Family.** What kind of family you were reared in helped shape your values and goals. Christ was reared in Godly home by Godly parents. The result – a Godly man. Being brought up in some homes; single parent family, foster care, relatives – life's lesson is estrangement from natural order.

Life's lesson teaches us that any man or woman who fathers a child or births a child, should be responsible enough to help navigate that child through life's lessons. Even God knew the possibility of broken families. *Psalms 27:10* tells us God will parent us through life's lessons when we are forsaken by parties that should have been responsible enough to guide us and teach us the fear admonition of the person and things of God.

Life's lessons can be hard, unfair, even unjust. But these classrooms can lead to success if applied and studied well. Take Joseph for example. Right out of the gate his family discredited him, even sold him into slavery. Wow, what a life's lesson. But the lesson learned here is the blessin'. What they meant for evil, God got the glory out of it. Joseph didn't drop out of life's classroom because it was unfair or too tough for him, he just continued to believe God and take the class until graduated Summa-Cum Laude. Talk about success! Just read Genesis 37-45. Life's lessons have a way of working themselves out. *Romans 8:28* tells us just that.

Life's lessons are to be learned. God the teacher, us the students – the lesson we learn will benefit us in more ways than one.

Life's lesson should be faced with faith, hope, courage, and expectation because the student will learn even in spite of him or herself. The eraser of flaws and mistakes will help each student fill in the blanks. Not rewrite the script – only God can do that. So enjoy the lesson. Remember ***the Lesson is the Blessin'.***

# CHAPTER 27

# TOO BUSY (BUSY-HOLIC)

Ministry requires more than knowledge, it requires work also. You've heard of a work-a-holic, what about a busy-holic. I mean, just too busy for even God. How do I know about a busy-holic? I've been there. Busy-holics seem to think the job can't get done without their signature. The busy-holic makes a long list of excuses why they just can't stop. Remember Mary & Martha. Read *St. Luke 10:40.* The busy-holics favorite sign ought to be placed out front in neon lights: No Vacancy.

You see, busy-holics seem to be restless, tense overworked, underpaid; always the driver, never the passenger. True, being busy can be a good thing, but not to the point where there is no pause, no rest, just work, work and more work.

Jesus has a remedy for the busy-holic in *Matthew 11:28.* It's the perfect prescription. If we just take it to the Great Physician He will give us the right dose.

Jesus was not a busy-holic – no sir. He rested always. What causes busy-holics – well, busy-holics are not usually patient. They want patience, but they don't have it nearly as much as they need it.

Busy-holics love fast food – burgers, fries, sodas. A busy-holics diet consists of fast prayer, fast church, fast fellowship; but is not the 'fast' God calls for. God calls for a spiritual diet, a *piece* of mind. *Isaiah 26:3* 'I will keep his mind in perfect peace whose mind is stayed on all'. A piece of contentment. 1ˢᵗ *Timothy 6:6* A covenant with Godliness is great gain. A piece of peace. Hebrews 12:14 Follow peace with all men and holiness without which no man shall see the Lord.

Busy-holics do have their share of honest ambition. They can never be accused of being bystanders, or idle, lazy, or ne'er doers. A busy-holics motto could be people that do things get things done. Busy-holics need to find a pace in God's timing and be led of the spirit, because not <u>all doing</u> is good. Busy-holics need to find out what needs to be done right now, what needs to be done later or what needs to wait. Jesus called a few busy-holics; Peter was always anxious for action.

The Bible says in Ecclesiastes 9:10 Whatsoever thy hand findeth to do, do it with all thy might. Busy-holics would do themselves a great favor if they meditated on *Isaiah 40:31* – Wait on the Lord and He shall renew thy strength.

# CHAPTER 28

# HUMILITY COUNTS

Humility is one of the greatest attributes one can possess. Some seem to have a 'leg up' on the situation, but some don't have a leg to stand on when it comes to humility. Humility is a modest or low-profile view of ones own importance.

I've heard it said, how can one be humble when they're so perfect in every way? When one is a true disciple or learner of Christ, ones own personal gifts, talents, education, physical appearance, financial status – these count as dung, as Paul said.

One cannot learn when one thinks they already know everything. Many people in higher positions whether secular or spiritual, often get caught up on titles. You must remember – a title means little, a testimony means much. I am not down-playing any earned status or position, but Christ himself said 'I came not to do my own will but the will of my Father.' True humility.

Humility can be achieved many ways. One way is to be humiliated. *Proverbs 16:18* says Pride goeth before destruction and a haughty spirit before a fall.

Christ used the illustration of placing a child in the midst of a group and stated, except you come as a child, you cannot enter the kingdom.

Humility, true humility, shows a dependence on God and respect for other people. What God desires most is not outward sacrifices, but a humble spirit. *Psalms 51:17*

Obedience to God shows humility. People who possess humility do not look down on others no matter where they are in life. Humility is the opposite of arrogance, or a 'puffed-up' ego. When one is humble they don't have to voice it, it emanates from their person.

Jesus was the epitome of humility. When a person desires to go up in life, the true way up is the way down (lying prostrate before God or kneeling before Him) with an open mind, heart, ears and spirit to learn what God is trying to tell us. Humble is an attribute that is better than gold or silver. It is precious in the sight of God.

Humility can be acquired along life's highway. If a person is willing to adapt to experience, mentorship, learn from his or her mistakes, the prize of humility can be had. I would love to say it is a virtue of mine, but it's not. I truly desire to acquire it in this life, but I am still in classrooms right now.

People seem to really love and appreciate someone who has this gift. We can grow and develop into being a truly humble being with the help of God Almighty. Jesus exemplified humility. At all times in extreme situations, in confrontation situations, he remained humble. I believe the more we develop the fruit of the spirit talked about in Ephesians 5, we are on our way to Humility Avenue. While we desire and strive for the most necessary gift, we must allow the God of all flesh to have His way in us and through us, and keep *Romans 8:28* in the forefront.

# CHAPTER 29

# HELP IS AVAILABLE

Help is a must for everyone. As you tread the path of life you will find yourself in need of some kind of help. No matter what your social status is, money, education, talents, family, everyone needs help now and again. Sometimes the enemy of help is pride, stupidity, arrogance, or just pure failure.

Help is needed when one cannot do something on their own. I'd like to thank God for allowing this simple word to be included in our vocabulary – HELP. I need help, you need help, we all need help. When God Almighty shaped Adam from the dust of the earth, knowing full well that man had the life of God in his innermost being; after God breathed life into him, his foresight for the man was Help. Genesis 2:7 and Genesis 2:18. Help was on the way. He needed help. Even though God was in the picture, he never left Adam. Man was in need of help for the task that was underway for him. Help for the task. That is what life is. It consists of task after task, and for about 99% of the tasks we face in life we need help. David talked about help in the Psalms on many occasions and even told us Psalm 121 where his help came from. It came from the Lord.

When we need help do we always know it? I doubt it. Sometimes because of our pride or false sense of self security, we don't realize we need help until it's too late. Many a marriage could have been saved, many an alcoholic could have been straightened out, many a drug addict could have been freed, if only they submitted to the difficult task of getting outside of themselves, out of their own thoughts and cried out I need help!

The lifeguard syndrome is a perfect example of someone who really needs help: even though drowning, the person fights and splashes in the water until some alert lifeguard dives in. Only when the so-called swimmer is worn-out he accepts the help offered to save his life. Life is like swimming. If you can't swim don't jump in the water, especially if there's no lifeguard around. I thank God for the times I've jumped in many pools, lakes, streams of life with deep waters raging, about to drown but I quickly realizes help was available. I called the lifeguard of all lifeguard – Jesus – and He pulled me to shore. I was sinking deep in sin, far from the peaceful shore; Jesus reached and pulled me in, never to sink anymore.

Love lifted me, love lifted me. When nothing else could help, love lifted me. The title of this book has help in it. You need some kind of help and hopefully one of these chapters has helped you so that you can be a help to yourself and others in any kind of situation.

Remember when a person is down and out, there are 2 things they will remember if they make it back up: The Hand that Helped them get back up, or the foot that tried to kick them or hold them down.

# CHAPTER 30

# HANDLING TRIALS

People often say trials come to make us strong. I found out there is also another reason trials come to us. If we are not prepared enough or equipped to withstand the pressure associated with the trial we will not survive, let alone come out victorious; or as Shadrach, Meshach and Abednego came out untarnished and without the smell of smoke upon them. Trials are most often God ordained but I also think we can place ourselves in trials that God never intended for us to be in. Remember Jesus' words in *Matthew 4:7*. Jesus told Satan, it is written, 'Do not put the Lord God to test'. Or simply put, do not place yourself out of God's umbrella of protection and think He will always protect you. This is Christ speaking these words here.

Trials show what you are made of; what kind of substance you have as a person. Remember the story of Big Bad Wolf and the Three Little Pigs. Wolf – Pigs. Wolf is hungry – pigs are innocent. The wolf comes to destroy their foundation and actually does it to two of them. One was built on a solid structure, so it lasted. What structure are you standing on when life takes aim at your peace, joy, health, family, or faith in a negative way? Will you be able to stand the test? How will you handle the request of – *I want a divorce* – or - *you have 3 months to live* – or – *your child is on drugs* – and so much more. *Matthew chapter 7* talks about the wise and foolish builders; sand verses rock. When the storms of life come crashing down, what is your foundation made of. Is it on the rock of Jesus or swaying sands of worldliness or substance abuse or pleasure seekers? If you are not standing on a solid foundation you will surely be doomed to destruction. But if you are built upon the word of God, then *Isaiah 54:17* will surely manifest in your trial. And whether the trial (or test) is fire, rain, wind, - you will be successful because God is your refuge, your shelter in a time of storm. Remember we are victorious even though we are faced with trials, the battle has already been won. So hold on to God's unchanging hand.

Jesus said, *I will never leave thee or forsake thee,* and *Be of good cheer; I have overcome the world and you shall also because I am your victory.* Are you in the fire now? Sometimes the only place you can see God is when you are in the fire!

Remember if you are His chosen one – His child – when you are in the fire He is also in there with you. So embrace *Isaiah 43:1-2* when facing and going through trials.

# CHAPTER 31

# WHAT TO DO WHEN YOU DON'T KNOW WHAT TO DO!

As believers we are sometimes cornered on our journey from earth to glory. When the Hebrew had left Egypt headed to Kadesh, Barnea or the Promised Land, they faced roadblocks, enemies **got lost** and wanted to stone their leader on a few occasions – only because they just didn't know what to do. Their leader did, but they refused to listen to him. The results were even more frustrating, because they didn't know what to do.

I think when our minds have gotten off of God and His leading, we get lost in our head and even get quite comfortable being lost. But eventually we want to move again and this is where surrender, humility and the Word comes up and you need to ask a question. Ask a question to who? Easy. Ask the same one who freed you out of bondage from those awful, paganistic Egyptians. When you have made the wrong turn in life, or exited at the wrong exit, it's okay to ask God to lead you in the right direction. David in *Psalms 119:33-37* asks God for lots of leading and asks him to turn him also. In life we make the wrong turns with bad decisions, a wrong relationship, a faulty investment, and find ourselves in a place called, ' I just don't know what to do'. This is when you simply just ask God in prayer. *'Lord I stretch my hands to thee, no other help I know, if you withdraw yourself from me where shall I go.'* Now you're being put back on the train tracks of Life 101. Remember you just jumped the tracks – a little derailing – you didn't crash because you would have been destroyed and unable to ask, 'What do I do now'.

God says, *Follow me, I am the way, the truth and the light.* Darkness is bad in the absence of light, so now I need some light or clarity of the direction I am needed in life, or I need some clarity on this life-changing decision I'm about to make. Jesus probably says, 'I thought you'd never ask'.

So now we know what to do. That is to seek God concerning all matters. When we seek others first; if it is a blind person and you are already lost or metaphorically blind – scripture says if the blind lead the blind they both shall fall in the ditch. So when you are at the junction or crossroads in life and don't know what to do, call on God and He will answer. *Jonah 1:1-2* – Jonah called on God and got an answer. He realized what to do in his dilemma. So should we call upon the Lord. While He is near seek His face early and be blessed.

# CHAPTER 32.

# THANK YOU

Giving and receiving thanks can be one of the greatest acts of benevolence or act of appreciation people can receive. *1st Thessalonians 5:18* tells us to constantly give thanks. 'Thank You' expresses ones thought of gratitude. There is not a person alive who has not at one time or another uttered these few meaningful words. We often sing a song in church – the lines simply say, 'Thank you Lord, I just want to thank you Lord'. We have many reasons to be thankful, especially for some things but they don't even know why they say it. Can you remember the last time you uttered these words or someone said them to you. How can you really argue with a thank you. I am so thankful every day.

Just stop and think about your very existence, your life – it deserves a thank you. No matter what situation you are in or have been in, a thank you always applies. In a bad or seemingly terrible situation, thank God it's not worse. It could always be worse. When sitting down reading the local newspaper or watching the news, when you realize that something good has happened in our country, it deserves a 'Thank you God'. Someone is in fatal car crash, 'Thank you Lord it wasn't me.' Thank you Lord for my health, strength, my very life deserves a *thank you*. God honors *thank yous* also. *John 6:11* Jesus gave thanks for the fish and loaves because God has supplied his need and the people's need.

I think when a person stops being thankful that is a bad place to be. I stop and begin to thank God and I run out of reasons why! As a matter of fact, whoever is living and in their right mind cannot help but be thankful. I am thanking Him at the moment of writing this because He has been so good and faithful to me. Thanks is not enough. Who can thank God more than for you. He is waiting for a praise, a praise of thanks. You're saying OK God, I'm OK. Okay, God I can make it a little further. Okay God I have just decided to give you constant thanks. Just think about it – why not give God thanks. You might say, thanks for what? Here are a few: You woke up this morning. How do I know that-because you're reading this (book). Is that a good enough clue? Legs working, arms working, hands picking up things, looking at the clock, walking, watching your children smile, on your way to work, food in your refrigerator, clothes on your back – is that enough? A 'Thank you God' is in order.

Thanks is the least expression I can show the keeper of the universe. Whenever I hear any kind of 'thank you', I know someone has just been blessed some kind of way.

When someone gives you a gift, thank you is in order. Someone helps you, thank you is in order. But the thank you to God should be *off the Richter scale*: God this is me the crown of your creation and I just want to thank you for your many blessings. God says what'd you say-Thank You. I am glad that you are committed to your creation. When I woke, oxygen was available for me to breathe; the sun was shining to light the world and provide energy. Somebody was cooking my breakfast, some cow was being milked for my cereal, some chicken was being plucked for my lunch, etc. Thank you is in order. Yes, thank you for the day – 12 hours sunlight, 12 hours night – after that the morning comes again and your red carpet of mercy is s[read out and renewed. Every day 'thank you' is in order.

…Leave out of my dwelling place, but before I leave, (Read Psalms 23) Thank you.

Walk to my car, or my horse, or my bicycle or motorcycle, 'thank you' is in order. Ride to my job (many people unemployed) 'thank you is in order. Arrived at work, (by the way, work is a blessing) get a paycheck at the end of the week… 'thank you'.

Listen, by now you should get the picture. *Psalms 107* says 'Give thanks to the Lord always. In every thing give thanks'. Thank You for Calvary.

Thank You for the Resurrection. Thank you for redemption. Thank You for St. John 14:1. Thank You for Jesus. Thank God for you. Thank You – I just can't say it enough. And if Sly could say it, he'd tell God "Thank you for letting' me be myself". Amen

# CHAPTER 33

# RACE CARD

Genesis 2:18-24

The Bible tells us in Genesis: God began to create a race of people. People are God's crown creation. He created them in His image and likeness. Now we discover man has the ability and capability to rule, lead or dominate every thing or being God has placed under their care. Who? Adam and Eve. He has specifically told them to be fruitful, meaning reproduce yourselves, prosper, be creative, thrive in the garden and the whole earth.

A race of people who not only had dominating godlike qualities, but did not know how to sin. Power over everything. The human race begins. In comes an outside force that was anti-God, that they as the human race even had power over. They were ignorant – didn't even realize their own abilities – and succumbed to the lie, and down went the human race.

Since the act of treason had been committed against their God, their creator, it was only natural for Adam, when called into accountability, to play the <u>Race Card</u>. Who else could he blame first for his own foibles? Not God, that came later. His own race – Eve – she must be the '*fall gal*. Ever notice how easy it is to play the race card? It all started with human injustice in the early Civil Rights Acts times. Black people were quick to play the race card when a seemingly injustice had been done to them. Just or unjust, let's play the race card.

But in the 21st century people who didn't look like them in color flipped the script and also began to play the race card. Double discriminate justice.

But the real race card is being exploited by Satan the devil. *Genesis*

*3:14* – The serpent is cursed and his job description is to eat the dust all the days of his life. Wait a minute, didn't God say in *Genesis 2:7*, Man was formed from the dust of the ground, and I think I just read it correctly-*Genesis 3:14* – Satan will eat dust all of his life. I see him eating the human race up one snack at a time. The real race. Get the picture? The race card is being played against us (fools). Satan is having his way with the human race and we're still playing with God and each other. It is time to reverse the race card on Satan and run the race as participants in the race, and represent not the human, but the supernatural human being. Time to stop the violence, sin, war and destruction. It can be done. Christ told some 'racers' in *St. Luke 10:19,* Behold I give you power over all the forces of the enemy.

It's time the race card worked out in our favor as a sanctified body of powerful believers, and play the race card of victory we have been given. The victory is already ours in Christ Jesus. The race we run as the super natural human race, we win in the end. Amen.

# CHAPTER 34

# THE GIFT OF MEMORY

## (REMEMBER)

*Genesis 8:1* is one of the most impacting scriptures to me – God remembers Noah. Memory or remembering. The dictionary says memory is a person's ability to remember things. Here in the passage of *Genesis 8:1* it says God remembered Noah. Wait a minute – you mean the God of the Universe can remember one individual? Wow. Noah gets God's attention and is catered to immediately.

Can you take just about 5 minutes and remember a few great moments in your life. I have the memory of an elephant (I've been told). My memory serves me well of my teenage years when I was rebellious and wayward, disobeying my parents way of life and forsaking my upbringing. But as I remember I still had a memory or reverence of God. One night in an alcohol and drug-induced state while around my peers; all so-called gangsters, criminals, pimps, armed robbers, "players", etc. One of my closest associates recalled how he had observed a Billy Graham book in my room at my parents' house. I was a little bit embarrassed to say the least. This was not the time or place to say such a thing. It was like preaching the Bible in a crap game. They don't mix. However, my memory serves me well, there was such a book in my room. I just hadn't discovered the power or meaning of the book. But now 45 years later looking back or remembering the reason for this moment, then *Proverbs 10:7* come to mind. It says the memory of the just is blessed. I was on my way even then in a den of iniquity and living a life of hedonism. God was imbedded in my heart. Thank God for my Momma, Grace Bennett, who raised us, weaned us on Christ Jesus. *Proverbs 22:6* was taking root right then and there.

God remembered me all these years later, as I look at our lives – His the prankster and me the victim of a cruel joke. I am now a saved, sanctified pastor, drug-free, crime-free, and He is still trying to get it right. One of the things I remember in remembering is, if God allows you get it right, it is your responsibility to keep it right. Get it right – keep it right.

As the song says: *'Memories light the corners of my mind'*, and God remembered me even in my mess.

How is your memory these days? Remember that God has remembered you, and you being His memory has you reading this treasure. As God remembers you, always remember Him. *Isaiah 26:3* Amen.

# CHAPTER 35

# FINALLY

*Ephesians 6:10* echoes these words: 'Finally, my brethren, be strong in the Lord and the power of His might. Put on the whole armor of God.' The apostle is writing this directive to people serving in the Ephesian church. His plea, his challenge – Be strong in the Lord. My plea – Be strong in the Lord *for real*. Why? Because we live in the 21st century and are facing an onslaught of chaos. Our planet now seems to be the headquarters for disaster: wars, economic woes, family decay, diseases rampant one after another, violence, climatic disaster. We must be strong in our faith that the creator God (*Genesis 1:1*) is totally in charge of all this seemingly mayhem. We have some power to make changes, but don't seem to be able to get the necessary unity of mankind to really keep any lasting change.

Remember the Civil Rights Movement? Change was made. The leader of it was martyred. Dr. King, just like Christ, was killed. When you stand for justice you are a target for the enemies. That's why you must be strong in the Lord _for real_, not for play or show or gain, but rooted in the strength of Jesus.

*Isaiah 9:6* says a child will be born unto us. The government will rest in his shoulders. He will be named Wonderful, Counselor, Mighty God, Everlasting Father, Prince of Peace.

Listen, with the way things are going now, what about teaching our youth to be strong in the Lord. They need a Way out. I'm not talking about religion. I'm talking about real live faith. Some of us do possess a measure of faith, but unless we release it to people who are faithless, it only serves for selfish gain. So we have to do as *Isaiah58:1* says we have to cry aloud and spare not because of the sins of our people. Are you a bystander to this madness taking place all over the world? Do you vote, do you pray, are you personally involved in community events. You'd better be, because the powers-that-be want to take your God-given rights and contain your very existence. I believe Jesus is the only solution for the chaos of the world. But what about the Jesus in us. Do you love your brethren? Love has action. Take notice of *Isaiah 5:20*. Please glean from this passage. It has a stunning wake-up call for us in the 21$^{st}$ century. Those of us who live under the sun. That includes ALL.

It says in *Isaiah 5:20*, How horrible it will be for those who call Evil good and Good evil. Let me help you to see the 'trick' for your destruction. You probably remember the old adage: *'If you can't beat them, join them'*.

The powers-that-be are making laws legalizing sin to our destruction, so that SIN is being made LEGAL. Look, you'd better wake up and smell the coffee. *Lev. 20:13, Lev. 18:22.* Legalizing same sex marriages which is strictly forbidden in the scriptures, legalizing drugs, already legalizing for your children to dishonor you by calling the police or outside authorities to come and deal with the parents because of house rules – This is chaos! We really need to be strong in the Lord and stand up to the evil system.

If not, we are doomed, and I cannot see that as the outcome of humanity.

# CHAPTER 36

# WHERE ARE WE HEADED?

I am talking about the current state of mankind. Where are we headed? Looking at the state of life's current condition, it looks to me that man has truly forgotten his maker and what He requires. In most cases – I'm not saying everyone – but the masses seem to have erased God from their memories. This seems to echo the words God spoke in *Isaiah Chapter 1 verses 1-10*. We, or the people of the world at large, seem to be on a crash course with God. A crash we will not survive. Take a look at the current world plight; anarchy, lawlessness, trouble, violence at an all-time high in the Middle East. Right here in America, urban homicide at an all-time high. People living alternate lifestyles, unnatural relationships, Russia and Korea are angry at anyone and everyone, our youth is tattoo crazy, and the dress code – young women exposing every raw part of their body, young men with their pants sagging ... I don't even believe there is such a thing as a dress code anymore. Nothing is appealing about carelessness or sloppiness. We are headed to a place of 'valuelessness' – no values in society.

Much of the music from the 70's & 80's pointed to this day of anarchy, Marvin Gaye uttered Michael Brown anthem in his song "Trouble", when he talked about trigger-happy policeman *'make you wanna holler'*. People are tired and frustrated at all of the civil unrest. I told the church we are called to obey the law, and I'm all for that, but what do you do when the law is wrong. Huh. Stand up – stand up for righteousness. We seem to be headed to disaster when it comes to human relationship. The Bible echoes in *Matthew 24:* Nation against Nation. That's going on now. Everyone is angry. Seems there is a murderous spirit rising up.

The direction we as people of planet Earth are headed is not a good place. No peace nowhere. The problem is us – mankind. We seem to have forgotten God's organic plan. *Luke 2 – Peace on Earth, Good Will Toward Men*, seems to have been forgotten.

I'm not talking about where are we headed when we die, bit where are we headed now. Plagues, the resurgence of Ebola, bedbugs, all kinds of strange phenomena that are not good have shown up at the door and we are not prepared to deal with it; water shortages, contaminated water, etc. Speaking of where are we headed, when crisis strikes or a major calamity that shuts down all communication, travel, etc., gold will not be important thing. Being famous or rich will not be the necessary thing, but bottled water and canned goods will be the new gold. You'd better stock up, I'm giving you some last day ***gold nugget*** info.

Stock up on candles, generators, water, canned goods and protection. Where we are headed you're going to need it. Just wait and see.

# CHAPTER 37

# SAVED

The Bible is the Book of Life for all forms of life that exist (mankind). The Bible states that God-the Creator of all-formed mankind from the dust or particles of the earth. *Genesis 2:7*. Formed by God and breathed into by The Almighty God himself. The man he has formed, now is alive and has the ability to be animated or functional receives a helper. *Genesis 2:20-25*. Now the man and woman are a team. A command had been given to Adam. I am quite sure Eve was made aware of the consequences of violating the command to obey God, the life giver. Simply, *Just Obey*. Chapter 3 verse 1 tells another life force called serpent. This creature was allowed to run interference between man & woman so God could see where their true loyalty was for the gift of life that had been bestowed upon them. They disobeyed God by violating His command and they fell from His purpose of living, and chose death over life. They have now become deformed by sin, or distorted, misshapen, or messed up, marred. God interacts in their dilemma and intercedes: death is a must, but grace and mercy will revive their current state. Until they return to the state, they must meet death. *Genesis 3:17*. But in the meantime God the author and giver of life, speaks the seed of Christ into the woman's womb and it germinates until the fullness of time. *Galatians 4:4-6*. Now when a child enters the present world a cry always accompanies every birth. This cry is for Daddy or Abba. *Galatians 4:6*. This cry is Daddy save me from this present condition.

Now in the fullness of time Matthew 1:21 comes into play. The same seed spoken of in Genesis 3:15 has come into the world to *save yes* **save** all mankind if they willingly accept the gift from God. Save them from their sins – a mandate. He shall save them (who?) his people, from their sins. How can he do this? Verse 23 says the same God that walked in the garden the day of the fall is walking again in this present age, saving those who would be saved. Saved from what, save from where…? People cannot be save unless they first come to the realization that they are lost. Saved from eternal expulsion from a holy life-giving, life-sustaining, life-keeping, life-supporting God.

People talk about when a person is in a critical illness situation, to put them on life support. There is only one life support. His name is JESUS. *John 1:1-4* states that life lies in the person of Christ. All of us who are saved had a quickening experience. *Ephesians 2:1.* Saved to not perish. Saved to glorify God. If you are saved you should know it. If you're saved and you know it clap your hands, I mean right now. If you're saved and you know it stomp your feet, I mean right now. Experience life. You have been formed by a holy God, deformed at one time by a wicked devil, and now saved by the Son of God. You have been transformed by Jesus. I you are reading this book; maybe by just picking it up out of curiosity, or given to read by someone else and you haven't been saved, right now you must realize that - #1 – you are a person that is alive. #2 – You will live life until you die. #3 – When you die the Bible says you have to report to God to meet your maker. *Bible reference Hebrews9:27.* When you meet Him, not If, but When, you will have to give an account of the life you lived on this earth. The most important question God will ask you about is not the life you lived, not how smart you were, what you accumulated while you lived, but, Do you know Jesus? Did you accept the sacrifice He gave for your life before you were born? If you are not save and want to make sure God will accept you into His kingdom forever, please repeat these words written:

*God I am a sinner. Please forgive me for all of my sins in my lifetime. I accept Jesus Christ as my Lord and Savior. I confess Him as the Lord of my life. I ask you Jesus to save me now. Upon the confession of my mouth and the belief in my heart, I personally receive Jesus as my Lord and Savior, Amen.*

You can pray this prayer and if anyone is near you who is unsaved, encourage them to do the same.

_____    _____

(Name)                                    Date of confession

# CHAPTER 38

# HAPPY SKILLED ORATOR

Romans 10:14-15

I previously penned a chapter about some styles of preaching, but I would be remiss if I didn't refer to the frame of mind, spirit and purpose of a preacher or spiritual public speaker, in this case, Christian speaker. The Apostle Paul mentioned the Act Of Faith being received by eloquent Godly lips of a spirit-filled preacher.

In chapter 10 of Romans verse 15 the Apostle speaks about Gift of the Orater or Preacher having been commissioned or sent by the God of the universe to communicate the nature, person, work and purpose of a preacher. One of the words Paul was is **'Glad'**. That word can be constituted as *'Happy'* in Acts 26:2.

When the Apostle Paul was preaching to King Agrippa he expressed the state of mind he was in to share with the king about his God.

I believe every preacher should be in a glad, happy state of mind and spirit when he or she is delivering a message from God about God to God's creation.

King David expressed how his mind was when he was going to hear the preached word in Psalm 122:1. When you have the opportunity to communicate God's word we should be joyful and full of zeal to tell the lost and also those who have received the new birth, the word delivered just life the newsboy tells his customers – *'Extra, extra, read all about it'*; not **'it'** but **'who'** – **God**. Not 'it' but the miracle of a God who cares enough about His creation to watch, manage, sustain and speak to the living creation He so loved in John 3:16. So He, God, speaks to His prophet, evangelist, pastor, teacher and tells us to speak a word much like a centurion requested of Christ in Matthew 8:8. He said speak a word only and my servant shall be healed. Preach the Word with gladness, and expectation and God will do as He stated in Jeremiah 1:12.

(Isaiah 55:6-11) **Preach on Preachers**

God expects us to preach the *Good News* in spite of whatever condition we are faced with. Ezekiel had just experienced losing the love of his life in Chapter 224 of his book and God commanded him to continue to preach (verses 15-19). Our job is the greatest vocation on the planet Earth and we should be glad to be a voice in these last and evil days to a disobedient and rebellious people. Who better to inform the people of a loving, just God than the preacher. Preach on.

# CHAPTER 39

# HOW TO HELP MAINTAIN UNITY IN THE CHURCH COMMUNITY

Psalm 133:1

My fellow yoke men, unity is a must in the family of God. Unity is not easy to maintain. Unity calls for action amongst all parties involved.

Unity takes discipline, inspiration, love honesty, and I believe with all of my heart, the last mentioned *Fruit of the Spirit* in Galatians 5:23: temperance of self-control.

Again the Apostle Paul tells us that a minister must be accountable to the Word. (Romans 6:11-14). The Apostle admonished the church at Corinth to unify. We are the Body of Christ and when and body part is disrupted the whole body experiences discomfort.

We as believers are to love one another. In the Book of John Jesus tell His disciples in John 13:34-35 people will see the Spirit of Christ when we love one another. We are to put aside petty differences, and strife, so we can keep unity in the Body of Christ. In the Matthew 18 Jesus saw schism in the body and He gave us a remedy to rid the body of disunity.

The Church is built upon Christ, but the people who come in the church are hurt, lost, sinful creatures and they must experience (2 Cor. 5:17). That scripture tells us of the birth of a New Creature, but this creature must be changed in the process of time. Church discipline is a must. God has called His people to togetherness. If we look at Proverbs 6:6,

God uses one of the smallest creatures to show us the benefits of unity; the positive effects that unity can have on a people. James chapter 3:14 reminds the people of God that envy and strife is not from God but from the Devil, who comes to cause division and disunity. So we are to strive for unity to build up the family of God, to promote healthy environment and we can come to one in the faith and conquer any foe before us.

# CHAPTER 40

# THE POWER OF A GOOD TESTIMONY

Hebrews 11:5

The patriarch Enoch had an awesome testimony. It is stated he walked with God. His testimony was that he associated himself with God; his walk and life was proof of his character.

Our testimony shows our past, present and future. We are to be examples to a world of people who need God's true proof. The testimony we live and give should reflect Christ and His power. When we confess Christ we should let our walk equal our talk. When God fills us with His word and spirit we are New Creatures and should show the power of Christ in us. A tattoo is the work of an artist, a song is the work of a songstress or singer. Our testimonies should reflect the inner person. Jesus said 'Let your light so shine that men may see it and glorify God'. When one has a good testimony their reputation precedes them. The Apostle Paul had associated himself with Christ so much, that when news became public that he was coming in the area, the noise of his presence caused people to take sick loved ones and place them in the middle of the street, so at the very presence of his shadow could fall upon any inflicted person and they could immediately be healed. What a testimony! What if your testimony carried that much power? God could really be glorified!

A good testimony causes others to have faith not only in God but a hope for their lives, no matter how messed it has been. So live a life worth glorifying God.

Walk before God in His ways in His commandments. The presence of you and the life you are is your testimony. Testimonies can also be added. David, for instance, started out as a sheepherder and became the great king that he was. As he was walking in the purpose to his testimony he developed a few flaws. But a plea to God restored him in his holy relationship with a Holy God. Walk upright at all times.

# CHAPTER 41

# THE GIFT OF GIVING

St. Luke 6:38

The word *Gift* is a powerful word. It is associated with the act of giving. Giving means to turn over or release something one has in their possession. To have the ability to give is a blessing. When you choose to transfer wealth, knowledge, love friendship, the Gospel, or yield a gift it is a good act. Sometimes it can be just an act of random kindness. That's what I like about the phrase when they tell us to 'Pay It Forward'. Total strangers – people who are in need receive something from someone – it makes a big difference. God the Father is the perfect example of the ultimate giver. HE sits on the circle of eternity, (says Isaiah 40:22) and in His observation looked upon the condition of humanity and saw the need, so sent help to a troubled, sinful mass of humanity and proceeded to act out with His gift of His son to save the world. (John 3:16)

Everyone is not a giver and especially having the gift of giving, I have the gift to give any and everything I possess so much that there have been times I have gotten in God's way. Giving is a good thing but to give when directed by the Holy Spirit is the best and most pleasant way to use that gift. God blessed Abraham with a son, Hannah with a son, Moses with the rod, Christ with his anointing. Giving is to be done without any expectation in the world. Real giving – it should come from the heart. 2 Cor. 9:6-7 tells us the repercussion of giving.

If you choose to give little, your return will be little. If you give plentifully your return will be bountiful, because God loves a cheerful giver. The widow in Luke gave all that she had to glorify God. An evangelist was preaching in an impoverished third-world country and when he made the plea to give, everyone came and gave their dollars and coins. In the meantime, a lad about 9 years old came forward and motioned for the speaker to place the basket on the floor into which he proceeded to step in to. How awesome! He was simply stating, 'I don't have any money, but take me, take my service. I am willing to give just what I have.'

# CHAPTER 42

# TIME

Ecc. Chapter 3

Time is one of the most valuable things we have at our disposal. Many of us don't appreciate or respect time but we must realize, as it is said, time waits for no one. Time does a lot of things. It marches on, it changes things, it brings light, darkness, it has the ability to be a fortune teller. In saying this, I mean sometimes we don't know a thing or so, but in the process of time we will understand it better by and by.

Time has different effects on different situations. For instance, in the principle of birth, it is a 9 month time process in life. Just think, in this world time runs out, time ends. There are two places where clocks or time managers are suspiciously hidden away. One is Las Vegas and the other is in front of the church. Why? Because if the people that were there saw them, it would change their whole frame of mind. Ask yourself the question, what does time mean to you, what have you chosen to do with your time, or what are you doing with the time you have now?

Time is the chronological sequence of life and its meaning in scripture, God is not governed by time because He is the Lord of time. We living under the sun are however governed by time. Just think – watches, clocks, sundials, night, day – these all play a significant role in time. People always ask what time is it. But the question is, what time are you talking about – the day, the reason, the season... The Bible frequently mentions the process of time or fullness of time brings about changes. People die in the process of time because of sin and not to have the ability to steal eternal life.

We measure time by seconds, minutes, hours, days, years. God is different. Remember a day is as a thousand years with the Lord. Usually a person's days or time have more drama than pleasure, whether rich or poor, old or young, check Genesis 47:9, Job &;1, 7:16; Psalms 144:4.

I know this time should be sacred, priceless and definitely appreciated because under the sun, it runs out.

# CHAPTER 43

# FINALITY OF OUCH

The chapter entitled 'Ouch' was birthed out of the thought of physical, emotional and mental. The word ouch usually comes from expressing pain. There is a saying, No Pain, No Gain. Pain is as real as breathing in this life.

There is another word called 'Hurt'. Combine hurt and pain, you get ouch. Job is such an example of life. We see he felt pain and suffering much like us. Some ouches come out of self-inflicted endeavors. God did not tell us we wouldn't experience any ouches in life but to expect them. Splinter in hand causes ouch response, broken heart causes ouch marathon. Jesus said 'let not your heart be troubled'. He was well aware we would have heart trouble. But it is the ouches of life that causes us to cry out to God (Psalms 40:1-3). In David's ouch dilemma, he cried out to God and God responded by hearing his cry, lifting him, reestablished his glory.

Ouches come from emotional disappointments. They come from bad choices. They also come from disobedience; refusing to give in. Pride causes ouches. What is the remedy for the ouches we make. It is reaching out to a loving God. There is a balm in Gilead and any other place when life hurts we go to the healer, who is Christ, We will experience hurt, pain, ouch. But Psalms 38 says many – I mean many- are the afflictions of the righteous, but God delivers from them all. We recently lost a great Kobe Bryant. But upon investigation he was dealing with a terrible ouch. Not being able to communicate with his parents for 3 years over a disagreement. How sad, when we experience the ouches that life seems to offer God always has a remedy – prayer- an anointed vessel – that vessel could be you. But call God, reach out and touch His word. Another brother or sister in similar situation. I have experiences many ouches, but I have trust issues, so I pray push them to the side and the person we push away usually has what we need for our current ouch situation. This is the real medicine man. Ouches come and go as long as you live, but wait and pray.

*Plop, plop, fizz, fizz, Oh what a relief it is,* when someone takes the spiritual to calm our messed up mind. Amazingly not always, not sinful, just stupid, short fuse, ego – eased God out, but God stuck. Let's let the ouches be. Acceptance is the key. Differences in our communities, racism, ignorance, sexism. I have been called to be a mediator or *Mister Fix-It.* Is your ouch loud (?), but I want you to know it doesn't have to be. Understanding, humility, family, are real for healing.

Learn to do this and the ouches will slowly began to disappear. Laughter makes the heart new.

What do we really want? Love, joy, peace, happiness. Ouches can heal, as a matter of fact they will heal. Let's love, pray, work in the vineyard. Let's take it to our streets. Not the ouch, but Jesus. Not the ouch, but fellowship. Not the ouch, but repentance. Not the ouch, but Matthew 18:15-17. We want healings, godly results. I am looking for results. Jesus said, Come unto me and I will give you rest.

God Bless You and see you in eternity.

Amen

Printed in the United States
By Bookmasters